Growing Small

How to Manage, Market and Measure
Your Way to Retail Success in 90 days!
Even if You Have No Time or Money.

Angel Cicerone

authorHOUSE®

AuthorHouse™
1663 Liberty Drive
Bloomington, IN 47403
www.authorhouse.com
Phone: 1 (800) 839-8640

Published by AuthorHouse   04/15/2015

ISBN: 978-1-5049-0391-2 (sc)
ISBN: 978-1-5049-0390-5 (e)

Print information available on the last page.

Contents

Acknowledgements ix

Author's Note xi

Chapter 1   What Am I Getting In To?...................................1

Chapter 2   Small But Mighty...7

MODULE# 1   Manage 17

Chapter 3   You, The Entrepreneur.......................................19

Chapter 4   Managing Your Concept.....................................24

Chapter 5   Managing Your Brand...33

Chapter 6   Managing Your Finances And Data 41

Chapter 7   Managing Your Team 54

Chapter 8   Managing Yourself...69

MODULE# 2   Market 73

Chapter 9   What Exactly Is Marketing?................................75

Chapter 10   The Foundation Of Your Plan: Knowing Your Customer.... 84

Chapter 11 Understanding Your Competition.....................................89

Chapter 12 Marketing From The Inside Out......................................93

Chapter 13 Sorting Out The Online Marketing Toolbox................113

Chapter 14 The Online Tools..119

Chapter 15 Traditional Advertising...157

Chapter 16 Promotions And Events..173

Chapter 17 Public Relations...190

Chapter 18 The People Factor..195

Chapter 19 Customer Service...203

Chapter 20 Two More Things To Think About..............................209

MODULE# 3   Measure...213

Chapter 21 Test. Measure. Tweak. Repeat. 215

Chapter 22 The What, When and How of Measuring.....................218

Chapter 23 Creating The Plan..231

Chapter 24 Before You Sign That Lease!..242

Chapter 25 Final Thoughts on Growing Small................................249

About the Author...251

Dedicated to all the small store owners who allowed me to come into their lives and turn them upside down in the name of success.

Acknowledgements

Thanks to everyone who took the time and had the patience to help me through this process. The whole concept of my business would have never even been possible without a serendipitous stream of events that started with Terri Echarte's networking group that Beth Linzner (a quarter-century long source of support) insisted I go to just one more time and where Beth Azor and Rachel Wein lit the spark for what is now, Tenant Mentorship. Thanks to you all!

To Ron Wheeler for taking a chance on a new idea with a thousand percent belief in me and its viability.

To Brenda Gonzalez, a bottomless pool of love, support and encouragement and a darn good proofreader!

To Brandon Hawthorne who, upon my request, allows me to spin out of control and without judgment, bring me back to sanity again.

To Marta Tracy for her friendship and the inspiration for the name Growing Small.

To Mae Greenwald and Bud Clark for taking the time out of their busy lives to read the book and offer suggestions.

To my family, Francine, Elizabeth and Catherine, for never doubting for a minute I could do anything I wanted.

Author's Note

Since you've made an investment of money to buy this book and will, hopefully, make an investment of time to use the information in it to help grow your business, I think it's only fair I tell you about myself beyond the perfunctory book jacket bio.

I have a passion for small business. It's in my DNA. As a child, I was always creating business ideas. My father was an entrepreneur (although they didn't use that word in those days). Despite the fact he had a family to support, he quit his job and opened a business in the detached garage of our home. There was no Internet or email back then. Not even a separate phone line. I remember he strung a clothesline from the house to the garage with a cowbell so my mother could ring him when he got a call on the home phone. I grew up seeing firsthand the ebb and flow of small business ownership. The good and the bad. The celebrations and the despair. Somehow, it fascinated rather than frightened me.

The desire to start my own business was always strong and in my mid-twenties, I opened an advertising agency. Later, I founded a newspaper. Although I've had some terrific experiences in the corporate world during my career, my heart was always in doing it my own way; forging my own path.

During those early business ownership years, thanks in part to my youth and inexperience, I can safely say I made every mistake in the book. My goal was simply to never make the same mistake twice, a lesson I always tried to impart to my employees. Because I was in a creative business, I never wanted to limit a team member's ability to innovate. Mistakes and missteps were part of that process. I learned early on to reward risk taking, even if it didn't always pay off. Somehow it all worked and helped us produce exceptional work and kept everyone motivated.

I also learned – the hard way- the importance of creating a solid foundation on which to grow: of being small and solid. My head was so filled with big dreams and aspirations I sometimes forgot to focus on the here and now. I had that entrepreneurial optimism, that inner voice that says, *"Everything will be ok."* I tried to grow too fast and sometimes paid the price for taking that path. Fortunately, I had people around me to pull me back to earth from time to time.

My fascination with business has served me well. I was deeply interested in how my clients ran their businesses; how they made money and created enterprise. I adored learning about what they did and how they did it from the inside out. Helping them reach their goals became my niche and ultimately helped me meet my own business goals.

Most of my career was focused on helping small-to medium sized companies on the business–to-business side. I rarely worked with retail or any consumer-facing clients. A few years back, when I was working as a business development consultant, I joined a networking group at the invitation of a friend. There, I introduced a new business idea I was considering. It was during the recession when so many people were literally forced to start businesses because there were no jobs available. My thought was to create a program that could quickly and affordably help small businesses launch and succeed. The challenge was to bring value to small companies that were limited in time and money.

Fortunately for me, some brilliant colleagues in the retail real estate business attending that meeting suggested adapting the idea specifically for mom and pop retail stores. The economy was really hitting this sector hard.

A great idea, yes. But I had no experience working with retailers. It got me wondering though. Was there a way to take the principles I successfully used with business-to-business clients and apply them to the retail world? I decided to give it a try - and so, my newest venture was born.

My company, Tenant Mentorship, created a platform designed to quickly and efficiently assess struggling independent retailers, identify their issues and create realistic plans to get them back to whole. The catch? Well, there were two. The first, it had to happen in 90 days because that was about all the life they had left in them. The second was the turnaround had to be accomplished without spending any money because there was simply none available!

What a learning experience and what a revelation! Yes, those principles did apply! Using them, I was able to help relatively desperate small retail and restaurant owners grow their revenues between 10 and 200 percent in a short 90-day period, not to mention address other management and infrastructural issues that were holding them back.

With some coaching and compassion, retail owners who were paralyzed by fear and a severe shortage of capital were able to come back to life. What a gratifying and creative way to earn a living for someone who adored small business success!

As my roster of retail and restaurant clients across the country grew, I began noticing disturbing patterns. While the economy certainly wasn't making it easy for owners to keep their heads above water, it wasn't the only culprit. There were key issues and mistakes common to most of my clients that were preventing seemingly viable businesses from enjoying success.

It occurred to me that it was time to change the conversation. Instead of discussing growth and the future, it was time to focus on the importance of creating a solid small business in the present – to grow small.

Growing small became my manifesto. After all, independent small business is the foundation of our economic machine. So why not focus on creating the best small business possible. Not bigger. Just better.

This book is based on the real issues, the real solutions and the real life success stories of small retailers and restaurants who successfully grew small. It's about owners who found themselves in a firestorm of debt, confusion and fear, yet applied these principles to go from bad to bold. It's about companies just starting out, who were able to create solid launch programs that positioned them for realistic success. It's also about my personal journey and the wonderful people I've worked with who put their fears aside and trusted that there might be a better way. These were people who, in many cases, had their life savings on the line and nowhere to turn. Their stories are an inspiration and the advice contained in these pages is proven to work and can help you at any stage of business ownership. Business can be better and it can be better for you – with improvement in as little as 90 days -- no cash required. If they can do it, so can you!

CHAPTER 1

What Am I Getting In To?

You're reading this book for a reason. Maybe you're stuck. Maybe you're just in the planning stages of your retail adventure. Maybe you started your business pre-recession and can't seem to recover. Or you opened post-recession and are having trouble navigating the ever-changing retail environment. Maybe you're just curious. Whatever the reason, you want to succeed and investing in a 90-day program to do just that seemed reasonable.

You're biggest question at this point is undoubtedly, *"How can this book help me?"* I'll tell you.

My method for working with independent retailers and restaurants is proven to work and I am going to help you recreate that process through this book. We'll do it together with a combination of honest assessments, education, real life stories for inspiration, lots of ideas to jump start the process, completing a series of exercises and finally, creating a 90-day plan to address your specific issues and goals. That plan will help you to create the unique breakthroughs in your business you've been seeking. I know because it has worked for my clients time and time again!

Even more exciting is the fact that the process will not just help solidify your business, it will also help you experience the joys of entrepreneurship again! After all, didn't you start a business to reap the benefits of operating independently and controlling your own destiny? It's time to do just that.

The *Growing Small* system is grounded in three major principles: Manage. Market. Measure. There is no magic bullet. There's work involved. But I promise I will lead you on a logical path to help you understand what needs to be done and how to do it.

Remember, this book is not a primer that gives you a basic look at all aspects of retail. Rather, *Growing Small* digs deep into actual experiences curated out of the most common questions, complaints and problems I've encountered with real life retailers in real life situations. And, of course, it provides real life solutions. It's the fastest way I know to solve problems once and for all and move on.

Before we move forward, please go to www.tenantmentorship.com/ growingsmallworksheet to download your free copy of the Growing Small worksheet. You'll be using it while you read.

Here's what we'll be covering in the book:

In the first chapter, Small But Mighty, we'll discuss why the commitment to growing small is the first step in creating the best, most profitable enterprise possible.

> **What I'll give you**: The advantages of growing small and a reality check on what issues might be blocking your success.
>
> **What you'll do:** Take an honest assessment of your business and yourself as an operator.

The rest of the book is divided into three main modules.

Module #1 - Manage

You can't build a successful business without properly managing key areas. Even a small house needs a solid foundation.

> **What I'll give you**
> A look at entrepreneurial pitfalls and how to overcome them as well as details on the five essential aspects of your business you MUST manage to achieve success.
>
> **What you'll do**
> Complete the Building Block and Action Item exercises outlined in each chapter to help you prepare to create your plan.

Module #2 -Marketing

Once you've laid the groundwork, you can start the process of attracting new customers. In the Marketing Module, we'll discuss the best techniques for getting the right people in the door, providing them with a great experience and getting them to come back.

What I'll give you

A better understanding of the marketing options that make sense for small retailers and how to use them to make your store unforgettable.

What you'll do

Follow along with the worksheet, indicate the areas which need improvement and identify the options that will work within your time, budget, expertise and goal parameters.

Module #3 - Measure

The Measure Module is the linchpin to the whole process. It's not enough to know if you're making–or not making–money. You need to know the how, when and why of making it!

What I'll give you

The power behind measuring your efforts and simple ways to ensure you know the effectiveness of every ounce of time and every dollar spent on your store.

What you'll do

Use this information to create a measurement device for each element of your 90-day plan.

Creating your plan

The final section of this book is a step-by-step guide to creating your 90-day plan. I'll show you how to pull together your top priorities and create strategies around them using the plan template. From there, you're ready to launch and measure!

Remember as you read, the purpose of *Growing Small* is to:
- Help you take back control of your business and its success
- Provide education about and solutions for the most common problems facing independent retailers today
- Hold a mirror to your business reality so you can reflect honestly on your issues and challenges
- Create realistic expectations
- Offer proven ideas for inspiration
- Help and encourage you to create and implement your own 90-day plan

As you read:

Pay careful attention to the case studies and stories
Let them inspire you. They include success stories – and failures. Learn from both.

Keep an open mind
While reading, you may think, *"I already tried that and it didn't work."* Or, *"That seems so basic."* Instead, ask yourself, *"Where is better possible?"* The truth is, the problems you think you have may not really be the problems at all. One thing's for sure, whatever's going on, you need to approach it differently. As Albert Einstein said, "We can't solve problems using the same kind of thinking we used when we created them."

Don't get discouraged or defensive. If you find you are doing something that might be hurting your business, don't feel badly. Get ready to fix it. Use this process as an opportunity to look at your business with a fresh set of eyes.

Let the creative juices flow
Jot down any and all ideas you might have while you're reading. Don't wait until you begin your plan. Think freely during this process. We'll edit your ideas later.

Small changes. Big results.
Understand that sometimes, seemingly little things can make the biggest difference. A client once said to me, "You're trying to shoot an elephant with a pellet gun." He didn't understand that success is made up of many small steps. Keep your expectations realistic during the process.

No matter where you are in the business life cycle – from start up to celebrating a milestone anniversary, you will find ideas and advice to help you grow small and grow smart. By dedicating the time to reading this book and creating your own 90-day plan, you can fashion the type of best-in-class operation you've always imagined!

CHAPTER 2

Small But Mighty

Most people want bigger. Bigger is, after all, the gold standard. We assume bigger means more money, less worry and less work. While I'm an advocate of growing business, I know that bigger brings with it its own set of risks and problems, especially when the growth is born out of the desire to be big for big's sake, rather than a legitimate platform for growth.

We want to believe in overnight success but unfortunately, that just isn't the case for most of us. Except for the extremely lucky, innovative or well-timed entrepreneur, most of us have to grow the old fashioned way.

I have seen too many owners who, having met with some success, begin to float on the expansion cloud.
I'll take the space next door.
I'll open a second location.

Or how about the entrepreneur who signs up to buy three franchises in a market before they even get the first one open? It's generally a recipe for heartache.

A few good months, or even a great year, does not necessarily provide the foundation to expand. I've seen good operators with successful businesses open a second location and expect it will have the same growth trajectory as the first. That's like having two children and expecting them to turn out exactly the same. It just doesn't happen. Each business is a living organism with its own personality and needs.

So for now, make the commitment to grow small. To become a "best-in-class" operator. To make your store or restaurant the most memorable and profitable enterprise it can be. To enjoy the privileges that come with owning a strong independent business.

The advantages of growing small

Control
When you focus on growing small, you maintain control of every aspect of your business as you prove your concept and hone your management skills. You won't lose sight of potential issues or any big opportunities.

Time to learn
No matter how experienced you might be, a retail or restaurant owner needs time to learn the nuances of their particular business in their particular location with their particular concept. This doesn't happen overnight.

Being nimble

Today's business environment demands ongoing change and evolution. You have to constantly try new things – new products, new merchandising, new marketing. You have the ability to turn on a dime, be innovative and hop on trends in the early stages. The big guys can't do that.

Less stress

Growing small offers the opportunity to manage excellence without the burden of paralyzing payroll and expenses. By carefully managing your growth, you foster a more creative and opportunistic environment, not to mention a less stressful one.

Focus and dedication

Growing small means putting all your energy into a singular goal. If you have one foot in your business and another in expansion, you're straddling a slippery slope of distractions. When you dedicate yourself to reaching small business stability, you will more likely achieve success.

Once your business is small and mighty, you have lots of options. This is certainly not true of those who expand too fast and find themselves in a money-losing proposition.

A small but mighty business owner can:

     Increase his/her salary

     Sell the business

     Work less

Sound good? Okay, it's time to dream big and start growing small.

Reality Check

One of the first things my clients say about me is that I'm direct. That's the polite way of saying I'm mean. Some have actually called me brutal. Others have cried during our consultations. Sorry guys.

I'm not mean but I am focused -- on you. I am totally, one hundred percent on your side. My job is to shake you out of your fear, complacency, stubbornness or whatever is getting in the way of your success and get you to the safety zone.

In some cases, my clients are dangerously close to losing their life savings, not to mention their dreams and hope for the future - and their sanity. I need to work fast, push hard and get them back to better in 90 days.

So I pull no punches with them – or with you. It's time to do a reality check and have an honest conversation about what's right and wrong with your business and your talents as an operator. They handled it and I know you can too. Put egos aside. Reality is not always a great place, but it's a great place to start.

During my initial consultations with clients, I typically hear some iteration of the following:

> *There's not enough traffic in this shopping center to support my business.*
> *The landlord needs to promote this shopping center more.*
> *The people who come here aren't my clients.*
> *I need more signage and the landlord won't give it to me.*
> *The economy/rent is killing me.*
> *I chose the wrong location.*

Placing blame has become a sport with small business owners, especially since the recession. A bad economy is a great excuse for a failing business. *"Hey, everyone's failing so it must not be my fault."* There's comfort in being part of this club. But it also means you've given up.

When I ask, "So what have you been doing to improve business?" I get the blank stare. The future success of your store is your problem. Yours and yours alone. Time to man up and look at what's really going on.

I was asked to work with an experienced salon owner who opened a beautiful new shop that was doing less than stellar numbers. When I went in for our initial consultation and explained that I could help her improve in 90 days, she was totally resistant. (Yes, she cried.) She had gone heavily in debt to build out the salon and in her mind, the only solution to her problem involved the bank consolidating her loans and the landlord giving her rent relief – neither of which was happening. She was also extremely disappointed in her staff, saying employees weren't stepping up to the plate to help her bring in new clients. She was scared, disappointed and frustrated. She also said she didn't want to work with me. What?

She asked to think about it overnight, which she did, and called me the next day and said, "Successful people do what unsuccessful people don't. I'm ready to get to work." She opened her mind to new solutions and made a commitment to grow small. She became, perhaps, my greatest success story. And by the way, she never got that rent relief or loan consolidation.

BUILDING BLOCK #1

Assessment

Please take some time to create a business and personal assessment. Write your answers on the Growing Small worksheet.

Business assessment

I don't have a written marketing or business plan.

My store is out-of-date, unattractive, dirty, or poorly merchandised.

I consistently have too much or too little inventory.

I don't participate in my business like I used to.

I don't truly understand business finances.

I tend to think big picture and don't pay attention to the details like I should.

My store concept isn't working because it's stale, irrelevant or too general.

Our customer service could be better.

I am distracted by personal issues (i.e. divorce, health, etc.).

I am afraid of my business failing.

I'm not sure of my target audience.

I do not have a POS system or I underutilize my POS system.

I don't have adequate insurance.

I have cash flow issues.

My business isn't providing something better, different or more fun than can be found on the Internet or at the competition.

My top 3 business issues are:

    1.

    2.

    3.

My top 3 business strengths are:
1.
2.
3.

Your personal inventory

The same traits and qualities that make entrepreneurs successful are also the qualities that can derail them. Where do you rank?

Vision

Do you have a clear vision for your business?
Is that vision flexible enough to allow you to see the need for change and evolution?

Passion

Passion for your business drives its success. It can also cloud judgment.
Is your passion getting in the way of making sound business decisions?

Impatience

A sense of urgency serves the entrepreneur well. Does your impatience keep you on track or is it creating unrealistic expectations and timetables?

Optimism

Thinking everything will be okay and actually doing what it takes to make everything okay are two entirely different things. Are you able to take off the rose-colored glasses when necessary?

Planning
Are you rigid in your planning or are you able to handle the bumps in the road?

Big picture thinking
Entrepreneurs love concepts and ideas. Are you operating at bird's eye level too often and ignoring the details?

Goals
What is the ultimate goal for your business?
    Grow it and sell?
    Hand it off to your kids?
    Earn a good living?
    Work less?
    Other? _____
Financial goals
How much do you want to sell annually?
How much do you want to earn annually?

Harsh realities

Before we move forward, this assessment, or future chapters of this book, may reveal you've made some mistakes….big ones. Issues like bad hires, vague concepts, taking on too much debt or creating a concept that simply doesn't work. Many issues can potentially be fixed. But what if you find that you really did choose the wrong location? What if the center traffic really doesn't support your rent?

Take responsibility. Try to get a rent reduction. Create your 90-day plan to show the landlord you have a solid strategy to fix the problems – quickly. Maybe it's time to pull together a modified or different concept that might work better at your location.

If you are convinced your business will never work, ask the landlord to find a replacement tenant. Be communicative. Remember, the landlord is not your business partner and may not agree to this, but in some cases will try to help struggling tenants get out of a disastrous situation as gracefully as possible.

Hopefully, you've taken your time with this chapter and made an honest assessment of your strengths and weaknesses. Armed with this, we can move forward.

MODULE #1

MANAGE

CHAPTER 3

You, The Entrepreneur

Let's start with the million dollar question. Why did you start your business in the first place? Did you:

- Identify a void or a niche in the market?
- Have an idea for a new or unique retail or restaurant concept?
- Have a skill set around which you could build a business? (hairdresser, clothing designer, jewelry maker)
- Enjoy success in a particular field and wanted to parlay that
- success into your own business? (insurance broker, chiropractor, chef)
- Find a franchise concept that interested you?
- Have a strong desire to take control of your destiny?
- Get downsized from a corporate job?

Whatever brings you to the table, congratulations! You're on the journey of a lifetime. And as a member of the retail owner's club, there's a pretty good chance that you, like most of your comrades, are faced with two major challenges:

An unbalanced skill set
Entrepreneurs are called upon to know every aspect of business. The experience and background you bring to your retail venture has probably prepared you to excel in certain areas but not others. Most of us simply don't know it all. To add to that, there are certain parts of business we like better than others. And some we find just plain distasteful.

Maybe you:
- Know how to design and manufacture clothing but don't know how to hire and train well
- Love merchandising your store but find dealing with payroll or inventory confusing
- Enjoy serving your customers but cringe at the thought of marketing

Whatever your strengths and weaknesses as a store owner, you need to do things outside of your comfort zone and knowledge base with a certain level of proficiency.

Difficulty keeping the CEO hat on
The minutiae of day-to-day operations can distance us from high level thinking. It's hard to wear the many hats of a small business owner and still maintain the CEO perspective so critical for keeping business from becoming reactionary and vulnerable. Even if you're a business of one, you're still the leader and your CEO hat must provide the filter through which you process all decisions.

These are the big entrepreneurial potholes everyone faces. Being aware of them and understanding that you are not "lacking" is the first step to growing small. There are many moving parts to running a company and as an owner, it's likely you're straddling many functions. I defy anyone to think big while scheduling employees, ordering inventory or even cleaning the bathrooms! It's your superhuman task to look at your business from a bird's eye level and still pay attention to the details. Granted, you may have employees to whom you can delegate some of the more mundane tasks, but you still have to manage those, making sure the work is done on time and always looking for better and more efficient performance.

Regardless of your likes and dislikes, skills or lack thereof, it's time to learn to manage each specific area of your business separately and as part of the whole. By using this book to help you think at a high level and then creating a plan to guide you through the details, you'll be able to keep yourself on the CEO track and function fully as a skilled manager.

ACTION ITEM #1
Key Management Skills
Please complete on the worksheet

List the things you like best and least about business ownership. Using the list of skills below, rate each of them in respect to your performance as Good, Needs Improvement or Urgent on your worksheet.

> Managing people
> Training/Motivating staff
> Hiring/Firing
> Marketing
> Social Media
> Financials and bookkeeping
> Scheduling
> Inventory Management
> Purchasing
> Merchandising
> Customer service
> Problem solving
> Planning
> Organization
> Prioritizing
> Creative thinking

The Big 5

In this module, we'll discuss the key areas a retail or restaurant owner must manage well. As you read the list, you may say, *"How can I possibly take on this many more tasks? Impossible!"* Trust me when I tell you that if you put the work in now, your daily life will actually become easier. In the long run, better management skills will help your business run more smoothly while giving you the confidence to make better decisions.

There are 5 specific areas of your business you need to manage for good health and sustainability. They are:

1. Your Concept
2. Your Finances and Data
3. Your Team
4. Your Brand
5. Yourself

In the following chapters, we'll talk about how managing each of these areas properly will allow you to focus less on the day-to-day and more on being great.

CHAPTER 4

Managing Your Concept

Think back to the day you had the notion for your retail store or restaurant. It was pretty exciting, wasn't it? You had a beautiful brain blip that spurred an idea worth pursuing. Maybe you were inspired to expand on an existing retail idea, doing it better or cheaper or putting your own unique spin on it. Maybe you conceived something totally new in the marketplace. However it came to you, it became the basic foundation for your business. A concept might be:

- A casual dining restaurant that specializes in healthier versions of traditional Mexican food
- A gift shop featuring one-of-a-kind items made from sea glass
- A coffee shop featuring organic beans freshly roasted on the premises

Your concept needs, first and foremost, to be based on a solid business model and make sense financially. Quite simply, it has to be appealing to enough people to be able to pay expenses (and at some point, produce a profit) based on realistic revenue expectations.

A concept is the starting point for your business and whether you've been open for a decade or just starting out, let's make sure your conceptual foundation is strong and ready to grow small. Having a well-defined concept makes small and large decisions so much easier because you know the exact framework and context in which you're making those decisions.

Once you've defined the concept, the next step is to create the vision - your mind's eye view of what your business will look, feel, smell and taste like. From that vision, you can thoughtfully execute the concept into a physical reality.

Let's take our healthy Mexican restaurant mentioned above as an example. As a business, it has the ability to capitalize on two important market trends:

> The popularity of Mexican food
>
> A move towards healthier eating

The concept is to provide a cozy, neighborhood, family-friendly establishment that provides great tasting, healthier versions of traditional Mexican food at a price under $13 per dinner entrée. The vision is to delight customers not just by serving great food, but by employing a professional, personable staff, well-trained in the nutritional benefits of your menu and in providing family fun. You can actually feel the experience the guests will have from the greeting they'll receive when they walk in the door to the delicious aroma of freshly made food. You can see the décor: multi-colored chairs sitting around hand painted tables, crisp staff uniforms, colorful plates of food, even hear the contemporary music with a Latin beat!

By having a well-thought out concept, decisions on execution become simple and straightforward because you know exactly what you're trying to accomplish. However, sometimes we make compromises that dilute the original vision. Again, using our Mexican restaurant, here are some ways the owners might have been detoured from proper execution.

> The hand painted tables in the original plan were expensive so the owner chose a more generic, less expensive option.
>
> In an effort to please a wider range of people, the owner added an array of dishes to the menu that were neither healthy nor Mexican.
>
> Adding these additional food options necessitated changing the menu. The owner didn't want to incur the expense of reprinting but rather, substituted plastic covers with computer printed inserts.
>
> Poor hiring practices resulted in high staff turnover and compromised the owner's ability to train properly. Customer service standards, as originally imagined, were not enforced.

As you can see, day-by-day, decision by decision, it's easy to chip away at the integrity of your concept. Any one of these decisions might not make a huge difference, but together they dilute the customer experience and the owner ends up with a generic – and potentially less successful – version of the business originally imagined. By not having a vision – or not properly executing your vision - you take your business from extraordinary to ordinary. And in today's retail environment, ordinary just doesn't cut it.

If you don't have a clear concept or vision, or your execution has fallen short, don't feel badly. The majority of my clients have been in the same position. I can't tell you how many of them honestly couldn't define their store concept.

I worked with a first time operator to open a new local spa. Spas, as you know, are high-touch, high atmosphere facilities in which music, lighting, scent and service are critical elements. We go to spas to relax, get pampered and be transported out of our everyday lives into a place of serenity. The owner had neither the vision nor the money to create this type of atmosphere but signed a lease to do just that.

The spa was located across from a very popular gym – a great source of potential customers synching perfectly with the spa lifestyle. As the facility was under construction, the owner invited gym members to a series of open houses in an attempt to generate pre-sales of spa packages and badly needed cash flow. Instead of creating a beautiful reception area (the rest of the facility was a construction zone) as a preview and teaser to build excitement of what was to come, she put an old desk in the lobby, opened a bottle of wine and somehow expected guests to be magically transported. No surprise, it didn't work. Her lack of vision and a severe shortage of cash actually put her out of business before she even had a chance to open.

I can also tell you about a candy store run by a gentleman who wanted to parlay his experience with an international chocolate brand into a high-end, homemade, artisan chocolate store selling beautifully packaged works of candy art to discriminating buyers. He was about a year in when the recession hit. He got scared and his immediate knee jerk reaction was to go to what I call the "Jesus and Jellybeans" concept. (This refers jokingly to velvet paintings and all manner of small things, like candy, that retailers will stock in an attempt to increase sales.)

When I first visited his store it was a hot mess – packed to the gills with an entire wall of penny candy including, literally, jellybeans. He squeezed in gelato and espresso counters. He began offering extremely unprofitable candy making classes (high labor costs) and added more and more display cases, taking away the charm and the high-end feel of the store. His original artisan candy was relegated to one small case, displayed in a way that did not draw attention, much less support the expensive pricing.

Over time, we cut. Cut the penny candy, (not as profitable as the homemade) cut the classes, eliminated the big bulky counters - even changed the name to reflect the focus on artisan chocolates. He recommitted to the concept of selling extraordinary chocolates and guess what happened? By putting aside his fear and executing his original vision, sales – and profitability – increased month after month.

Dilution vs. Evolution

So you've got your concept solidified and executed. Unfortunately, you're not done. And this is where it gets tricky. In today's fast-moving retail environment, concepts get old and stale rather quickly. It's critical to know when it's time to change or adapt your vision. Trends spring up overnight. Tastes change. The economy gets better - or worse. Competition increases. Populations shift. There are hundreds of valid reasons to evolve.

How do you know when it's time? It could be due to an unexpected, yet major milestone event: competition moves in across the street or you lose your chef. It could be that traffic and sales are declining despite all reasonable efforts, indicating the market may have grown weary of your offerings. These events necessitate changes to ensure continued success.

The best time to take a hard look at your concept and vision is at the peak of success. When things are going as well as you could ever imagine, it's time to evaluate how to best evolve to meet the needs of today's fickle consumer.

A healthy small business is always looking at the next step or it might go the way of the great city clubs of the past. Remember them? City clubs opened decades ago as places for businessmen (yes, men) to gather, network, be seen and conduct business meetings punctuated with sizzling steaks, scotch and cigars. They were generally located in a downtown neighborhood on the top floor of a prestigious office tower. Their target audience was just a short walk or an elevator ride away. Companies paid annual dues for membership plus a monthly fee for which they received solicitous service and recognition. Membership in a city club was the hallmark of prestige in certain business communities in the latter half of the 20th century.

But things changed. Companies began moving to suburban locations to save money and reduce commuting time for their employees. Food trends changed. People began experimenting more with ethnic cuisines and the trend of lighter, healthier eating began to take hold. More women entered the executive suite and in the early days, weren't as comfortable or, in some cases, even welcome into these dark, mahogany good old boy clubs. There were a thousand changes going on in every community but the city clubs turned a blind eye.

The final nail in the city club coffin was the recession. Club memberships were slashed from budgets as companies struggled to stay in business or desired to appear sensitive to the financial struggles of their employees. Memberships were viewed as unnecessary luxuries and city clubs began closing their doors across the country.

Here's what's so interesting about this story. There are still business people in every downtown, right? They're still eating lunch somewhere, right? And there's still very much a segment of the market that values a members-only environment. Was there really any reason for these clubs to close? If they had paid attention to what was going on in the world and evolved with the times, there's a chance many of them would still be here today. Just because something works for a long time, doesn't mean it's going to work forever. And stubbornly holding on to a vision can mark the death knell for a business.

Do you watch Project Runway or Top Chef on TV? These shows are definitely my guilty pleasures. I've watched both for years and definitely learned about competition by doing so. There are a lot of similarities in the two shows and the personalities of the contestants who compete and are eliminated week by week. The participants are selected not just for their talent, but for their unique points of view. At the end of each show their designs and dishes are critiqued by the judges. The winners, and those who go the furthest in the competition, generally receive the criticisms gracefully and the really smart participants take the comments to heart and try to make improvements in the next rounds. But there are always one or two contestants who fight back, saying something like, '*This is my vision,*" or "*I'm not going to stray from my vision.*" They shout about their "vision" endlessly in the confessionals. They hold on dearly to what they believe to be right. It is these very contestants who get eliminated fairly early in the season. Why? Because they are not even considering the fact that their visions may be lacking or inadequate or just plain wrong. They're not taking responsibility for the fact that maybe the judges are right. They're not even thinking that perhaps, with just a little tweaking, their vision could be extraordinary!

In the case of retail, your customers are the judges. Maybe they'll like your offerings. Maybe they won't. But one thing's for sure, if people aren't buying what you're selling, you need to listen to them. You can stubbornly stick to your vision or you can modify it to create a solid retail success and make it to the next round. Which would you rather do?

BUILDING BLOCK # 2
Concept and Vision
Please complete on the worksheet before moving forward.

What was/is your business concept?
Define it in one or two sentences. Be VERY specific. A women's clothing store is too general. A more defined concept might be a women's clothing store appealing to young professionals working in more conservative businesses with price points under $100.

A good concept is unique and targeted and sets you apart from the competition. It appeals to a certain target demographic. If you're not crystal clear about your concept, take some time to think it through and put it in writing on the worksheet.

Is your concept timely? Relevant? Is it well thought out?
Is it time for a change or modification?
Important tip – If your concept model is broken, don't put it back together again the same way!

What items on your original "dream" list got lost, forgotten or compromised?

Did their elimination impact the overall concept?

What are some of the internal or external factors that may cause your vision to change – now or in the future?

Does the physical reality of your store match your vision?

CHAPTER 5

Managing Your Brand

Branding is a word that gets bandied about a lot these days. It's sometimes confused with marketing. The American Marketing Association defines a retail brand as the identity associated with the goods and services you provide. Brand equity means that consumers are responding more favorably to you than the competition. Quite simply, your brand differentiates you from others in your category. I think this quote from Jeff Bezos, CEO of Amazon, explains it best. "Your brand is what people say about you when you are not in the room."

What goes in to a brand?
Retailer attributes that comprise a brand include:

> Products or services offered
> Physical store appearance and experience
> Quality of employees and customer service
> Price points
> Marketing message and consistency

Think of your brand as the pulse of your business. It's everything you stand for: a physical reflection and psychological perception of your store. It's not just your name or logo. Yes, these are components of a brand but branding goes far beyond these specific elements.

Branding isn't just reserved for Coke, Nike and Apple. A strong brand is essential for growing small as well. A unique and well-established brand creates a strong bond with its customers that can even help insulate it from certain economic influences.

Be warned. Just because you've been in business for a while doesn't mean you've established a brand identity. There's a mistaken perception that because a name has been out in the marketplace it's an established brand. Think about it. If you changed the name of your store tomorrow, would it really affect sales?

Building a brand involves your store experience, merchandise displays, packaging, your community involvement, employee professionalism, sales policies, reputation and integrity. It's the totality of your operation and its personality. If you're very good at building your brand, people will become emotionally attached and fiercely loyal to it.

A strong brand:
- Adds value to your business (This is especially important if you want to sell)
- Builds credibility and identifies you as the favorite with your target audience
- Is the foundation for expansion
- Says you have made an impact on the marketplace
- Eliminates the need to compete on a pure pricing play

ACTION ITEM #2
Your Brand

Which brands (national or local) do you admire?
What are the qualities of these brands you can emulate?

Building your brand

In the previous chapter you defined your concept. Now it's time to ask, what does that concept stand for? Value? Quality? Unrelenting customer service? A unique service or product? Social consciousness? Discounted pricing? Exclusivity? Made in the USA? Convenience? Environmentally friendly? We will be going into more specifics in the MARKETING MODULE about ways to build your brand, but for now, let's take a look at your business and evaluate your brand identity.

Does your merchandise or service and pricing match the brand message you are trying to convey?

One of my clients had a growing clothing store, nicely merchandised and filled with sports and dress clothing for the young professional woman. She built her brand on serving this customer. Unfortunately, she had some health issues and decided to let her very young staff participate in the buying decisions and as a result, ended up with a store full of very youthful and unsophisticated clothing. Sales plummeted and regular customers stayed away because they were no longer being served. The merchandise strayed from the original brand promise.

Is your brand message translated throughout your store? Is it easy to understand? Does it appeal to all the senses? Does your staff represent your brand? Are they trained properly? Are they pleasant? Informed? Courteous? Neat? Clean?

I work with a beautiful coffee shop that is warmly decorated with lux stools, plush couches and chairs. The owner created a comfortable meeting place for guests to enjoy sustainable, local coffee, wine and food. Her dynamic and high energy personality conveyed beautifully in her store. After the launch, she decided to spend less time on site and hired a manager who was neither high energy nor personable. The effect of his management style was immediate and devastating. Business declined. I secret shopped them three times in one week; twice during prime early morning hours. Each time, the store was empty and the employees were sullen. Chairs and couches that had been grouped for conversation were now haphazardly arranged. The lighting was dimmer. Everything was off. But what was really noticeable was the music. Each time I visited, the soundtrack playing was like a funeral dirge. On my third visit, I invited a client to meet me. Again, no other patrons, unhappy staff and that music! My client, who had never been there before, looked at me and said, "This place is depressing." The next day, I met with the owner to discuss the issues. She finally understood how these problems were stemming from the manager. I tried to have a discussion with him and he, rather unpleasantly, said he didn't have time to worry about things like music. He didn't understand how the neglect of these details was undermining this very new brand. Ultimately, he was fired. The owner hired more energetic staff and within weeks the entire atmosphere of the store changed. Life filled the place again. And the music? Pitch perfect!

Does your brand message offer a differentiator and a promise that separates you from the competition?

One client handcrafted leather and beaded wrap bracelets. She used the tag line "Leather and beaded wrap bracelets." Hardly a brand statement that inspired interest in an already competitive category. In discussing her business, I found she used connections from her previous career in television and was able to get stars and celebrities to be photographed wearing her jewelry. From that differentiator, we created her brand message, "The leather wrap designer to the stars!" That message was easy to translate and integrate into all her marketing and conveys a certain élan not existing in her competitors' brands.

Does your marketing reflect the brand message?
From your logo to your promotions, think of each marketing element as your voice, like it was you actually telling your brand story. That will help give it the personality and consistency necessary. If it doesn't sound like you, it probably isn't properly reflecting your business.

I recently went to a wine tasting seminar at a large, well known liquor and wine chain. The company built its brand on offering a huge selection, great pricing and knowledgeable, well-trained sales people. Every inch of the store beautifully reflects their brand message. Education via tasting classes is a part of their marketing strategy.

Everything about this tasting contradicted the store's brand. It started with an unappetizing presentation of meats and cheeses thrown onto a platter. The seminar leader proudly announced these foods were all available at the store. Given how they were displayed, who would want them? The seminar started late; the room was freezing. It wasn't an auspicious beginning. The seminar leader was unprepared for and uncomfortable with his presentation. He had not rehearsed or timed the program and halfway into the two hour session, we had only tasted 1 of the 8 wine selections scheduled. The sold out crowd got bored and demanded things move along more quickly. It wasn't pretty. By the time it was over- almost an hour later than scheduled - attendees actually bolted out of the room. I watched as one hundred percent of them left without buying anything – certainly not the desired outcome from the store perspective. As a marketing event, this was an epic fail and reflected badly on the brand.

Brand opportunities and enhancements

In creating a 360 degree branding experience, the devil is in the details. You may have taken care of the big stuff. Now let's have a look at the little things that send big messages.

The transaction

The way a product is wrapped or packaged speaks volumes about your brand. Plus, there's the added benefit that customers take that brand message home as a reminder. Is your merchandise leaving the store in a way that best represents you? Take a look at your receipts. Are they computer generated with your logo or at the very least, your store name and contact information? Or are they handwritten and hard to read? You brand needs to be reflected in every element of the sale.

An Italian restaurant I work with was focused on increasing its lunch delivery business to corporations in the area. I went to the restaurant one day around lunch time and saw a line of plastic grocery store bags on the counter. I thought it was garbage! Turns out, the truth was even worse than that. These were the corporate food deliveries! What a branding opportunity they were missing by not using lovely boxes or beautiful, logoed statement bags for their delivery orders!

Store policies

Is your return/exchange policy clear and customer friendly? I cringe when I see signs like this on a cash wrap: "NO exchanges. Store credit only." A more brand-appropriate approach would be, "We want you to be delighted with your purchase and are happy to exchange your merchandise for a store credit within 10 days of purchase."

More brand busters

- Unpleasant odors inside or near the rest rooms
- Dirty windows
- Handmade/taped/torn signage
- Employees with sloppy hair or dirty clothing
- No one answering the phone and/or a low energy voicemail message
- Not having the products or services you claim (We're out of that.)

A final word on brand busters - typos! I say this because, in my opinion, typos can bring any business down. I see them in brochures and ads, on social media postings and websites. Since I am the world's WORST proofreader I am sensitive to the problem. If you aren't good at proofreading, find some help.

When managing your brand, look at each individual element, identify any weakness or potential weakness and make a plan to fix it. It's up to you to manage your brand and protect it every day.

BUILDING BLOCK # 3
Brand evaluation
Please complete on the worksheet before moving forward.

What does my brand represent?

What emotion do I want to elicit when people think of my brand? (Fun, aspiration, love, happiness, nostalgia, power, safety, inclusion?)

What is my brand message?

How do I think customers perceive my brand?

How am I building my brand?

What is detracting from my brand?

CHAPTER 6

Managing Your Finances And Data

Information is power and never before has so much power been available to benefit retail business owners in the form of data. From the Internet to Point of Sale (POS) systems, you have unprecedented access to the information you need to run a successful business.

It's not enough to know you make money. You need to know HOW you make your money. Data and finances are inextricably linked in understanding and analyzing the best ways to grow small. Sadly, the vast majority of clients I work with do not use available data to their advantage. I get the *"It's all in my head,"* answer a lot when questioning a client about their business. Sound familiar? Think about that. How can you possibly run a business without understanding the how, when and why of your customers and sales? This data is a gift.

You don't have to be a CPA or an MBA to understand and benefit from financial and operational data. You do need to recognize there's a lot more to business than a profit and loss statement. You have to know your money. It's your money! Know your customers. They're your lifeblood! Know every nuance of your business. This is powerful stuff!

Here's the most amazing part. By understanding this data, you no longer have to guess about what inventory to buy, what customers to target or when to schedule staff. The answers are sitting right in your computer!

Even if the thought of analyzing data evokes a strong negative emotion, work with me here and trust that once you do this, you'll be hooked on the power this knowledge brings.

The very first thing I ask clients to do is track their Key Performance Indicators (KPIs). KPIs provide powerful insight that can help determine targeted marketing solutions, pricing strategies, scheduling and hiring needs, new revenue opportunities, inventory management and a host of other strategies that can easily result in increased revenue and decreased expenses.

If you don't already own a POS system, get one! The right POS is essentially a business in a box. Yes, it's possible to track most of the information manually but it's an extremely inefficient use of your time. With the advent of POS software available in the cloud, you no longer have to invest in expensive hardware. You can purchase the service of your choice at a very reasonable monthly fee that's relatively insignificant when compared to the advantages it can provide.

KPIs are as easy to track as the push of a button provided you have a good POS system and input information regularly and accurately. You can pull daily, weekly, monthly and year-over-year comparison reports.

But first, you need to know what you need to know – and why.

Below are the most commonly tracked retail KPIs with a description of each and real life examples of how these numbers can help you. While not all are applicable to every business, choose the ones that will benefit you.

Key Performance Indicators

Sales by time of day and day of week
By knowing exactly *when* you're selling – or not selling – you can create strategies to improve business during non-peak times, know when to run promotions and when to schedule employees – resulting in better service and potentially decreased labor costs.

A pizza restaurant was offering a daily lunch discount on weekdays. Upon analyzing the numbers, we found that Thursday and Friday lunches were triple the volume of Monday through Wednesday. There was no need to offer the discount on those days. By eliminating discounts on Thursday and Friday, sales stayed the same but the owner realized increased profitability.

A clothing store, upon tracking sales by time of day, realized the restaurant next door was throwing off great after-dinner traffic. They began opening later to avoid labor costs during virtually non-productive morning hours and staying open later to benefit from restaurant traffic. Sales, of course, went up.

Sales by category

This is simply a list of items sold by category. A clothing store might segment by tops, skirts, dresses; a restaurant by entrees, lunch/dinner, appetizers, beer and wine. The more specific, the better.

I worked with a pancake house that offered an extensive breakfast menu. They knew that pancakes were, by far, their most profitable item; meats generated the least profit. They had never pulled an itemized sales report and upon doing so, made an amazing discovery. Guess what they sold least? Pancakes! The most? Meats! That made it easy for us to create pancake-focused promotions and samplings. We also raised prices on sides of bacon, sausage and ham to keep in line with escalating costs. In no time at all, pancake sales were soaring – as was net profitability.

A clothing store's sales declined by over 40 percent. The owner had never pulled a sales by category report and when she did, it revealed most of the decline was in sales of dresses. It was like a lightning bolt hit! She had dropped two dress lines the previous quarter and never checked to see how that impacted her sales.

Average sale

By dividing your total sales by the number of transactions, you get the average sale per customer. This benchmarks what a typical customer spends and your goal is to always increase this number. Increasing the average check is the easiest way to raise revenues immediately!

A coffee shop needed to increase revenues by 10 percent or about $2000 a month. The owner was about to invest $6000 in advertising with the hopes of increasing traffic to achieve her revenue goal. By knowing her average sale, which was $3.95, we were able to bundle two items as a special (coffee and a cookie) at $4.75. Just by upselling her regular coffee customers to the special, she was able to reach her revenue goals without spending a dime on advertising.

Traffic/Sales conversion rate and sales per employee
One of the biggest complaints I get from owners, particularly those in suburban strip malls, is *"There's not enough traffic in this center."* And sometimes, quite frankly, there's not. A simple test will help you gauge exactly what's going on.

Track your daily walk-in traffic. Keep a spreadsheet at the cash wrap broken down by day of week and time of day; 9-11 am, 11am -1 pm, etc. Put a slash in the appropriate box each time someone walks through the door. Create another column for transactions and each time you make a sale, put a slash or the actual total of the sale.

At the end of 30 days, perform the following calculations:
Total traffic for the month

Total traffic by day of week (add up all the traffic for each Monday, Tuesday, etc. to see which are your busiest traffic days.)

Total traffic by time of day – add up all the traffic in each time block to determine the busiest times of day.

With this information, you can more effectively schedule labor and create promotions to help shore up sales on slower days.

Finally divide the total traffic for the month by the total number of transactions. For example:

Total traffic = 1500 per month

Total transactions = 250 per month

$$\frac{1500}{250} = 6$$

This means you're closing one out of every 6 customers that come into your store or have a sales conversion rate of slightly under 17 percent.

Let's examine these numbers

First, we know we had 1500 opportunities to make a sale this month. Most clients who complete this exercise are surprised at how much traffic really does walk through the doors. Secondly, we know we closed one-sixth, or less than 17 percent, of those walk-ins. What have we learned? If your closing ratio is less than 20-30 percent, your issue may not be lack of foot traffic at all. If people are visiting your store but not buying, I would encourage you to evaluate the competency of your sales staff as well as price points and merchandise mix. Power!

This ties right into sales per employee. Retail sales is just that...sales! Employees aren't there to simply ring up transactions or serve food. They are there to sell your products or services.

Shops that pay salaries, not commission, usually don't track this KPI. Some say it's not an accurate reflection because some employees only work part time, some work in peak periods and others during slower times. How do you make a fair evaluation?

First, total each employee's sales and divide by the number of hours worked. This will give you a sales per hour number for each individual employee. Now track these figures against themselves monthly. So, if Employee A starts at an average of $110 per hour in sales, track to see if those sales go up or down each month. This way, you are benchmarking them against themselves, not each other. If you find there's a truly significant discrepancy in these numbers it could indicate you have some weak links on your staff.

Hopefully, you are conducting regular sales training but if someone's sales are going down, you can intervene quickly to find the source of the problem and remedy it. Later, you can track these figures in year-over-year comparison.

One clothing store's sales had been steadily declining over a year's time. The owner was frequently absent and left the store in the hands of her manager who was also the primary salesperson. In researching the sales decline, we pulled the sales-by-employee report. Her manager's sales had gone down 47 percent year-over-year! Frighteningly, the owner didn't know this. Clearly the manager had become complacent and lost interest. The owner was able to fix the situation by better motivating and training her manager, giving her goals and incentives to sell more and keeping a closer eye on her. The manager's sales rose 25 percent in just 90 days.

New vs. repeat customers and frequency of purchase
Successfully growing small requires a good balance of new and repeat business. As I am fond of saying, there are two ways to make money

in retail – selling more to existing customers and bringing in a steady flow of new buyers. I've worked with many owners who proudly tell me the majority of their business is repeat. This is not necessarily a good thing. Neither is a lot of one-off customers. If you don't bring in new clientele, business will shrink. It they only come once and don't return, that signals a potential problem with your product, service or pricing. But you need to know what's going on so you can address it.

A beauty salon client did not track their new vs. existing clients or client retention KPI. Once they began tracking and analyzing their numbers, it was clear they were getting plenty of new clients, they just weren't retaining them. In the salon business, a customer isn't really isn't considered a customer until they've visited a minimum of three times. By understanding they had a client retention issue, we were able to implement a two-fold strategy that included customer service training for the stylists to insure greater satisfaction as well as a new customer welcome program that offered new clients discounts for pre-booking their next appointment.

Now that you know the makeup of your customer base, take a look at how often they frequent your store. Weekly? Monthly? Annually? By understanding shopping patterns, you can create targeted marketing strategies to gain additional sales from existing customers.

Let's take a restaurant for example. Out of a database of 1000, we found that 35 percent of their regular customers come in once a month. By pulling the average check for this group and the day of sale, we know the majority of these 350 people usually come on a Saturday night and spend an average of $40 per visit.

Knowing this, we did a couple of things:
- *Created a marketing campaign targeted specifically to these customers to invite them in for a mid-week special.*
- *By knowing the average check is $40, (with an average entree price of $15,) we knew they were largely parties of two that are ordering dinner but not drinking wine or liquor. We offered them special wine pricing to increase the average check.*

Lead sources

We'll be discussing how to analyze your marketing efforts in detail in the MEASURE MODULE, but in order to effectively measure your programs, you first need to be able to track them. Most POS systems offer the ability to enter codes that track back to coupons, promotions and ads. Be sure to code everything you do and enter that code with each corresponding sale. We'll discuss how this can be a huge benefit to your store later.

Customer profile/demographics

Getting an accurate read on your demographics helps you fine tune offers relevant to existing customers and gives you ideas for attracting new ones. Take the most basic demographic data- the zip code.

I worked with a day care franchisee for whom the franchisor did a quarterly direct mailing that was not producing results. In comparing the zip codes the franchisor used for the mailings against the actual zips of current students, we saw they were not synching. By adjusting the mailing zips, they were able to use a more geographically accurate database, thus producing better results from the marketing dollars spent.

Tracking your KPIs

You should pull your KPI reports, at minimum, weekly. Compare them to your monthly goal and to the same week's reports from last year. Look for early warning signs. If you pull your numbers at the end of the first week of the month and they're tracking down, look at traffic. Is it down? Why? What can you do to increase traffic for the rest of the month? Maybe you didn't have a promotion planned and now is the time to create one. Maybe traffic is good but your average sale is down. How about creating a tiered pricing special?

By understanding your numbers, you avoid the victim mentality. There's no reason to stand there at the end of the month saying, "*We had a bad month.*" With the proper information, you have the opportunity to be proactive and turn things around on the spot.

Of course, at the end of each month you should analyze your year-over-year KPIs. Has your mix of items selling changed? Is there any significant sales increase or decrease in a certain category? When you track KPI's and use them to better understand your business, you have truly taken control of your success.

Profit and Loss Statements

P&L's provide important information about the financial health of your business. Often times, small business owners don't want to invest in this expense but you do need to pull them, at a minimum, quarterly, but it's best to do it monthly and review them with your accountant. Review the current month, year-to-date and year-over-year comparisons for the same period.

A couple of key items you'll want to keep an eye on:

Gross profitability
Your total sales less the cost of goods sold equals gross profit. That margin needs to be healthy enough to support your business. Depending on the category of business, you could be looking at anywhere between 25 to 60 percent gross profitability. Conduct an Internet search on typical margins for your industry. If it's less, you either need to negotiate better pricing on your inventory or raise prices. Selling too many items at discounted prices can impact your gross margin negatively.

A shoe store I worked with provided me with P&L's that were shocking. Since sales weren't where they needed to be, the owner discounted her shoes at will just to make sales. Her gross margin was about 7 percent! At that low level of gross profitability, she had no hope of a sustainable business.

Labor and rent costs as a percentage of sales
Your rent as a percentage of sale, inclusive of Common Area Maintenance (CAM) charges, should be around 10 percent. If you are about to sign a lease, you should figure this number conservatively as it relates back to your forecasted sales. One of the biggest issues I find is retailers lease space that is either too big or too expensive for their concept. Perhaps they are overly optimistic about forecasted sales. Keep this number in mind as a barometer for your healthy business.

The correct payroll or labor as a percentage of sales, again, depends on your industry. It could range anywhere between 9 and 30 percent.

If you are hovering at or above the high end, you may have to adjust your payroll in order to achieve better profitability.

Now you know the value of managing your finances and data. Learn all the capabilities of your POS system to make the management of these tasks quick and easy. Take time to get the training and be sure to instruct your employees to input properly. Put yourself in the position of power by intimately understanding your business. I can tell you one thing with absolute certainty. Every time I work with a client and teach them how to track and analyze their numbers and data, they become hooked on the power and move forward with renewed confidence because they truly understand their business.

BUILDING BLOCK # 4
Your Finances and Data
Please complete on the worksheet before moving on.

What do you need to do regarding a POS system?
- Investigate purchasing one?
- Get the proper training to fully utilize your POS system?
- More complete entering of information?

Select the KPIs relevant to your business:
>Sales by Time of Day and Day of Week
>Sales by Category
>Traffic and Sales Conversion Rates
>New vs. Repeat Customers
>Frequency of Purchase
>Lead Sources
>Customer Demographic Information

If you haven't already, evaluate the gross profitability, rent and labor costs on your profit and loss statements. What areas need improvement?

CHAPTER 7

Managing Your Team

Whether you have a staff of one part timer or an entire team, employees can be a source of pride or cause irreparable damage to your brand and reputation. These are the folks that have daily interaction with your customers. They are the face of your store. Their professionalism - or lack thereof - is a direct reflection on you and your establishment.

Interestingly enough, the management of personnel often evokes even stronger negative emotions than technology or finance. Do you cringe at the thought of disciplining or firing an employee? Are you frustrated by their lack of initiative? Will you keep a marginal or bad employee longer than necessary just because you dread the thought of firing, interviewing, hiring and training?

Creating a good retail sales staff is particularly challenging since you are generally hiring unskilled or part time workers, often with little experience. High turnover rates are one of the biggest frustrations of retail and restaurant owners. But since you, the CEO, are also the head of human resources, assembling a stellar team is your responsibility.

It is possible to develop policies and procedures that not only help take the angst out of hiring and training, but also help your store develop a reputation of being a great place to work so quality people start seeking *you* out. A well-run team can absorb daily tasks making it possible for you to spend more time as the visionary CEO and leader of your company which will ultimately result in greater success.

First, manage your own expectations. One thing that really brings an owner down is disappointment in employees. We tend to take an employee's lack of commitment (or perceived lack) very personally. We expect our staff members to be as excited about and committed to our businesses with the same passion we feel. Unfortunately, that's rarely the case. Employees, even those heavily incentivized to succeed, are not owners and will almost always fall short of lofty expectations. So please, stop taking it personally. It's destructive and unproductive. Do start creating a dynamic sales team that operates at peak performance levels to help achieve your goals.

Let's talk about managing your employees in the following areas:

Hiring/Firing

Admit it, you probably don't do much about hiring until forced to; an employee quits, gets sick or needs to be terminated. Then…. panic! Your first impulse is to hire quickly, satisfied with a warm body rather than a quality employee. You pay for that decision over and over again in so many ways and keep that person around far too long because going through the hiring/training process AGAIN is just too much too handle.

It's not easy finding great employees, especially on short notice. That's why I recommend you consistently interview potential staff. Bring candidates in weekly or monthly. Keep the want ads running. Always be on the lookout out for quality people. No matter where you go, when you come across someone with a great personality or a spark, ask them if they'd like to come in for an interview. If someone refers a friend, conduct the interview even if you're fully staffed. By doing this, you create a potential employee pipeline which will take the urgency out of making hiring decisions when the situation arises.

This ongoing interviewing process also makes a strong statement to your existing employees. All too often, staff members believe they have us over a barrel. They think, sometimes rightly so, that regardless of their performance they won't be fired. They capitalize on an owner's distaste for the hiring process. By consistently – and publicly – interviewing, you let employees know you are serious about hiring the best team members and employees' jobs are only secure if they perform. It also gives your best staff members confidence in knowing you are serious about building an exceptional team. There is nothing worse for morale than holding employees to a double standard.

Tips for hiring and firing

Take your time

Even if you're desperate for help, take your time. Look for a great attitude over experience. You can teach process but you can't teach personality. Does the candidate seem genuinely engaged? Do they smile easily during the interview?

While that initial interview can give you a lot of insight, a trial day will speak volumes about a potential employee's capabilities. Offer your top candidates the opportunity to work a paid trial day and carefully observe them. The right choice will become abundantly clear when you do this.

Treat prospective employees with respect

Be sure to contact all candidates to let them know your hiring decision – even those who are rejected. Let them know kindly and honestly why they are not getting the job. Remember, they're potential customers and referral sources, too.

Fire right away

If your gut tells you the employee isn't a good fit, you're probably right. Fire them before you become resentful and they become toxic.

Creating a sales culture

The bottom line is the bottom line in retail. A successful retail store or restaurant is dependent on selling so it's imperative that you create a sales culture at your store. I'm a firm believer sales people should be rewarded for selling. Hire people who are motivated to reap the financial rewards of meeting and exceeding goals. I have found quite a bit of resistance about this from owners who think a commission-based program will encourage staff to become too aggressive and competitive. They fear it will create an unpleasant experience for customers. Let's be clear. You are not training staff to be used car salesmen. You are training them to sell which, quite simply, is providing the information a customer needs to make a buying decision. Selling is inviting prospects to participate in the opportunity you bring to the table. With proper training and a solid reward system, you can cultivate a great sales team as well as a great customer experience.

So whether you decide to implement a commission program or a monthly bonus program, create a reward system that will help you meet *your* goals. Rewards can be in the form of gift cards, merchandise or commissions. Just be sure the reward is commensurate with your product or service and the level of sales skill required.

Setting up a commission program

I have seen all types of commission programs in the retail world. They sometimes pay on meeting daily goals and sometimes just pay – regardless of whether an end goal is met. Neither of these structures help elevate sales levels and definitely don't inspire employees. Creating a goal and commission plan takes a bit of creativity and strategic thinking.

There are three key elements for setting up a successful incentive program:

1. Create monthly goals. I don't believe in daily goals. They are almost impossible to meet and a good rain storm could wipe out an employee's bonus potential and discourage them.

2. Be sure the total of the employee goals is *more* than the actual monthly revenue number you want to achieve.
3. Offer larger incentives for exceeding goals.

How does this play out? Let's use this scenario for the month of April.

The commissions used in these scenarios are just an example. The actual commission percentages you will pay should be based on your own store profitability and employee status.

Assume

Your sales staff includes: 1 fulltime manager and 2 part time sales people

Last year's April revenues:

Manager's sales	$28,000
Part time staff #1	$ 5,000
Part time staff #2	$ 7,000
Total – last April	$40,000

Note: Just count employee sales in this number – don't count your own.

Your goal for this April $48,000 (20% increase)

This year's April goals by employee:

Manager's sales	$35,000
Part time staff #1	$ 6,250
Part time staff #2	$ 8,750
Total sales goals	$50,000

> *The total of employee goals exceeds the actual April revenue goal of $48,000.*

Commission Structure

Manager

  2% on all sales up to goal ($35,000)

  5% on sales of $35,001 and above

  $250 for team hitting store sales goal of $50,000

Sales staff

  $100 bonus each for meeting sales goal

  An additional $100 each if they exceed goal by 20% or more

In this scenario you are paying the manager a regular commission on what she sells, and more importantly, incentivizing her to exceed her goal AND to motivate the staff to meet and exceed their goals as well.

Let's say the total sales for this April play out like this:

	Scenario 1	**Scenario 2**
Manager sales	$32,500	$37,500
Staff # 1	$ 3,500	$ 6,000
Staff #2	$ 8,750	$10,500
	$44,750	$54,000

Scenario 1

Total revenue is less than the actual revenue goal of $48,000 but still represents an 8 percent increase over last April.

The manager would earn 2% X $32,500 = $650
Staff # 1   no bonus
Staff # 2 $100
Total commissions and bonuses paid $750

Scenario 2

Total revenue exceeds the actual revenue goal of $48,000 and the employee revenue goal of $50,000.

The manager would earn $1150

2% X 35,000 =	$ 700
5% of $2,500 =	$ 125
Bonus for achieving store goal	$ 250
	$1,075
Staff # 1	no bonus
Staff # 2	$200
Total commissions and bonuses paid	$1,275

In scenario 2, you are paying out a mere $525 extra to achieve an additional $6,000 in revenue over and above your 20 percent year-over-year increase! To put it another way, you have paid $1,275 in commission to achieve a 35 percent increase in sales ($14,000) over last year. That's quite a deal! Plus, your employees feel more empowered because they had the opportunity to pad their paychecks!

Sales contests

You can choose to deliver rewards via a monthly contest, structured in a number of ways:

- Reward only the highest achieving employee
- Reward each individual who achieves their goal

- Reward each individual who achieves their goal ONLY if the overall monthly revenue goal is made

It's important to create a spirit of team competition to make this work. Track each employee's progress on a chart and be the head cheerleader in acknowledging progress on a regular basis. Be sure your contests or incentives are in line with your goals. For example, if you run a hair salon and have made a deal with a particular manufacturer for special pricing on shampoo, the contests should center around the sales of that shampoo. Alternatively, if you have an underperforming item, create an incentive around it.

Commission and rewards aren't simply a way to pay staff if they happen to meet goals. They are tools to insure that your staff's performance helps you achieve *your* goals. As you begin a reward program, give it a few months to let everyone get used to the system, get the proper training and work out the kinks. Let them know you are serious and they will we judged on their sales performance monthly. Once you pull the trigger, meet with each staff member at the end of every month to review performance and assign goals for the next month. Conduct a debrief session. Don't focus on what went wrong. Ask them what they think they did correctly and what they might have done differently or better. These are great learning opportunities.

Pay special attention to those employees who do not meet their goals and provide additional training to help them. If an employee is consistently underachieving (let's say 3 months running) and your efforts and training have not paid off, it's time to find someone new.

Training

It's not enough to create goals; you have to teach employees how to meet them! Without the proper training, you are just setting them up for failure and frustration.

Training is not simply a new hire orientation. It's an ongoing process in which you commit to providing your staff with the knowledge and tools they need to succeed.

Training tips
- Schedule training twice a month minimum. You can use one of the training sessions for discussing product knowledge and/or store systems, the second for sales techniques.
- Keep the trainings to a set amount of time, no more than 1 to 1 ½ hours, and stick to an agenda. It shows respect for your employees' time and lets them know you're serious.
- Enlist help. There's no need to do it all yourself. Ask vendors to train in product knowledge. Enlist an employee with a great performance record to conduct a sales training (this is a great motivator!). Bring in outside sales people to train. They don't have to be from the retail industry to impart terrific information. Learning sales from the perspective of a different industry can be enlightening and informative.

In addition to training on product knowledge and sales, here are additional items for your agenda:
- Product demonstration
- Suggestive selling
- Upselling

- Using the POS properly to gather customer intelligence and processing transactions quickly and efficiently
- Asking for emails and social media likes
- Your brand and what it represents
- Customer service

Role play different sales scenarios. Yes, your staff will complain and yes, they'll be uncomfortable. Over time, defenses will wear down and these sessions will become very productive.

If you're very good at selling, have employees shadow you with the specific purpose of observing your style. At the end of the shadow day, ask them to evaluate your performance and discuss what did – or didn't work– and why.

Define and assign

The easiest and best way to manage employees is by clear communication and expectations. I've seen owners who let bad employees "get away with murder" because they expect nothing more. They've given up. If you accurately define a job, deliver a clear job description, assign duties in detail, train properly and maintain an expectation of excellence for all employees, there's a good chance you'll get what you expect. By being clear, you are empowering your employees to do their job well.

What to do with the toxic employee?

Is there anything worse than an employee who is negative or unhappy? Doesn't it make you angry that you are actually paying these people out of your pocket when they're making you and everyone else miserable? Toxic employees can bring down morale and damage your reputation with employees and customers. Further, by keeping these people, it sends a message to the rest of your staff that you're willing to tolerate this type of behavior.

You're probably dying to get rid of *that* person, but sometimes, these truly negative people are also very good at their jobs. I've seen any number of situations in which a key employee is incredibly toxic but the owner is hesitant to fire them because they perform well or fill a difficult-to-replace position. In other words, you, the CEO, are operating out of fear and are being held hostage by this employee.

You only have two options when it comes to toxic employees:

> If it's not a key staff member, fire them sooner rather than later before you (and your staff) become so resentful it actually begins to hurt your business.

> If it is a key employee, begin interviewing immediately. Once you start talking to new people you'll see that you really do have better options. This will make you feel more confident and secure in your decision to replace the toxic person.

Remember the story about the coffee shop owner with the bad manager? He was brought in as an operational expert, an area in which the owner considered her skill set weak. Because of that, she was hesitant to replace him or even have discussions with him for fear he'd quit. By operating out of fear, she kept him on too long and allowed him to compromise her business. Once she began interviewing for his replacement and realized she had better options, it made the decision to release the manager easier and improved business on all fronts.

If you feel it's warranted, have an honest discussion with the toxic employee about the impact of their negativity on the business. Give him or her very specific goals and a timetable for changing, at which point they will be terminated if there is no improvement.

The blessings and curses of long term employees

What seems like a blessing to some can actually be a detriment. If you've been in business a long time, you may have a veteran staff. I've had clients where some – or most – of their staff members have been working with them for 5, 10, or more years. If you're experiencing high turnover, I'm sure you would love to be in this situation. But frankly, it has its own set of challenges. Because these veterans have demonstrated extreme loyalty and responsibility, owners may start to let things slide. They become hesitant to enforce rules and drop training classes because the tenured staff already "knows it all." They may get lax on dress codes and in general, feel pressure to turn the other cheek in fear these employees may quit. This isn't good for business and it certainly doesn't set a good example for new hires. If you have long term staff members, be sure they know they're valued and appreciated but hold them to the same standards as you would any employee.

Create a no-judgment zone

The iconic Tiffany 5th Avenue in New York City sees thousands of people walking through its doors daily. I'm certain the majority of these people are browsers. Nonetheless, each visitor is greeted warmly and given a brief overview of the layout of the store. It is almost assumed that everyone aspires to own something from Tiffany at some time in their lives. By creating an environment of inclusion, everyone feels like a valued customer even if they don't buy a thing.

Be very clear that employees are not to make snap judgments about any prospect. I find that often, staff members will make a quick determination about whether or not a person will actually buy the minute they walk through the door. Maybe it's the way they're dressed or they may seem distant and uninterested. Don't make the mistake of assuming these people will not buy – if not now, perhaps at another time. Show every customer the same respect and level of customer service.

Set up an "on call" system
A small shop or restaurant generally operates with a pretty lean staff which can cause chaos when someone calls in sick or needs to miss work for one reason or another. Try setting up an "on call" system to help alleviate this problem and insure you'll always have staff on hand. An "on call" system simply means that each employee agrees to be available to work certain days of the month when they would typically have off. Let's say, for example, you run a hardware store with 4 part time employees. Saturday is your busiest day and you must have at least 3 people on the floor to accommodate customers. Schedule each of your part timers with an "on call" Saturday meaning that once a month, they agree that if they receive a call from you by 10 am, they will come in to work. You'll sleep better at night knowing you have someone on reserve status.

A dynamic staff can be a great asset to your business, a source of pride and tremendous support in your efforts to grow small. Don't deny yourself the opportunity to assemble the best team possible.

ACTION ITEM #3
Managing employees
Answer these yes or no questions on the worksheet.

I have a bad or toxic employee that needs to be fired immediately.

The quality of my staff is not as good as it needs to be.

I need to implement a training program or improve an existing one.

I see the benefit of creating a performance-based incentive program and would like to implement one.

CHAPTER 8

Managing Yourself

As CEO of a growing small business, you will need to manage your own education, information flow, inspiration and passion. Being an effective leader means keeping yourself at the top of your game, not just in business but in spirit as well.

One of the traits identified in successful CEO's is something called "passionate curiosity." Coined by Neil Minow, co-founder of the Corporate Library, passionate curiosity is the desire to–the *need* to– know the how, the what and the why of everything. CEO's aren't necessarily the smartest people in the room but do have the strongest desire to learn. What if I did it a different way? How can I change it to make it better, faster, quicker, more profitable?

Are you passionately curious? Did you start your business with that deep, in-your-gut type of drive only to have it fade over time? The intensity of a long-term business commitment can erode passion:

the minutia of day-to-day operations, tough times and difficult employees can all cause energy to ebb.

The key to success through passionate curiosity is sustainability. What can you do to maintain high levels of passion for your business? First, take ownership of the fact that you are responsible for maintaining your passion. If you don't nurture yourself, it won't be hard to let employees, clients or colleagues suck you dry.

Make "What if?" your favorite question
What if I hired a different person to do that job? What if I bundled my products differently? What if I changed my work flow? Consistent questioning of your concept and processes will lead you to new and better solutions.

Don't work in a vacuum
Studies show adults produce 65 to 93 percent more ideas in groups. So find passion partners – (no, not that kind) or form an informal advisory board by identifying friends and colleagues who are, in your opinion, passionately curious. Preferably, they will come from different industries and backgrounds. Arrange to meet with them on a regular basis and use these meetings as forums where participants are invited to throw out the biggest, best and dumbest ideas. No judgments allowed. You'll all share tremendous energy and inspiration.

Allow yourself time away from the day-to-day minutia
The biggest killer of big thinking is the mundane. If you can, delegate some of the daily chores. If you can't, schedule time to get away from

them. Even if you take an hour a week to think quietly and create, you will reap the rewards.

Manage your expectations

Few things are more detrimental to success than expecting more than is realistically possible at a given moment in time. I have worked with owners who were doing quite well for their particular stage in business, but because they had such lofty expectations, always felt defeated.

Self-motivation and inspiration

There's a certain amount of isolation that goes along with being a business owner. You and you alone are responsible for the majority of the decision making and certainly the hard work of leading by example. It can lead to burn out. Business ownership is draining. You have to constantly replenish your soul with information and inspiration. Whether it's through reading, keeping a journal, practicing yoga or trying new experiments with your business, keep a constant flow of new information and experiences going that will help trigger ideas, creative energy and new perspectives. Create your touchstone by envisioning what your life will feel like when you have reached your business goals.

Get out of your store

Successful retail ownership requires a 360 degree view of the world. Since retail requires to you spend many hours in the store, it may prevent you from benefiting from different perspectives. So get out. Network. Join a community group. Go on field trips. See what the rest of the world looks like and use that new information to help grow your business.

Treat yourself with respect

You are, after all, the CEO. Treat yourself as well as you would someone who works for you. Be kind. Be complimentary. Be appreciative of all the things you do.

Being the top dog doesn't mean working like one. Commit to doing what it takes to keep your head clear and your passions ignited. No one wants to work for a crazy person. Least of all, you.

ACTION ITEM # 4
Managing Yourself
Answer these yes or no questions on the worksheet.

I am committed to acting like and treating myself like the CEO of my company.

I will commit to the following:
>   Finding passion partners
>   Creating an advisory board
>   Allocating a certain amount of time each week,
>   blocked in my calendar, to work on my business,
>   learn new things or get out of my store.

MODULE # 2
MARKET

CHAPTER 9

What Exactly Is Marketing?

Ah, the mysteries and misunderstandings of marketing! Is it advertising? Social media? Your website? Is it merchandising? Branding? Customer service? The answer is, "Yes!" Marketing is the amalgamation of all the techniques you use to get people in the door, provide them with a great experience and, of course, get them to come back.

Marketing is about making your business unforgettable. In a world of ordinary, creative marketing is the launching pad for exceptional. It gets people talking about you. It makes them curious. It engages them. It's your hook to pull people into the world you've created.

Here's a very cool example of being unforgettable. A restaurant owner put a sign out each day on one of his tables that said, "Reserved for the President of the U.S." When he would greet a group waiting to be seated he'd take them to that table and say, "Sit here. What the heck. He's not coming today." *How much fun did he create for his guests with that simple and silly gesture? Talk about customer experience!*

In a world where we look at marketing as an expensive and expansive discipline, we forget that it's the small, interesting, funny, unexpected and clever things we can do daily that add up to our ultimate success.

Marketing is about building a community. People get great satisfaction in discovering something new and wonderful. They take ownership of their find and, without even being asked, try to steer others to enjoy it as well. As your business's Chief Marketing Officer, you have the opportunity to bring together like-minded people who love and appreciate what you do.

Marketing is about delivering the right message, to the right people at the right time. Let me repeat that. Marketing is about delivering the right message to the right people at the right time.

Think about it. We receive tens of thousands of messages daily via TV, radio, newspapers and social media. It's a bit overwhelming to think our job as small business owners is to penetrate that big wall of noise and have our message break through. As impossible as it seems, it can be done.

One of the best examples of delivering the right message to the right people at the right time that I can offer is a simple one. I live in an urban area with doggie waste bag dispensers on almost every corner to insure you have what you need to keep the city clean. A very clever dog walking service simply taped their sign, "Need a dog walker? Contact us." to dispensers around the city. Fancy? Not so much. Clever? Without a doubt. They got their message out to exactly the right people at exactly the time they might be considering hiring a dog walker. I use this as an example to show how marketing your business can be truly effective, measurable and either cheap or free!

Marketing is about understanding the value of a loyal customer

We love to see new faces walk into our doors! After all, that's why we're in business. But creating a complete and seamless customer experience - and selling more to the people who already know and love your brand – is high on the priority list.

Marketing is not a luxury for small retailers

Every business, regardless of size, must build an effective marketing program. No excuses. No delays. If you don't, you'll be forced to compete on a pure price play. And that strategy, for a small business, is almost always a losing proposition.

The Marketing Discussion

When I begin talking to new clients about their marketing, I find there's generally confusion about advertising vs. marketing. *"I don't have any money for advertising,"* or *"Advertising doesn't work for me,"* are typical responses. Advertising is just one element on the marketing spectrum. Advertising is a part of marketing but marketing encompasses so much more. It has to do with everything from the greeting a customer receives when they walk in the door to an easy-to-navigate website. In other words, marketing is about the total customer experience.

I also hear a lot of this: *"I've been at this location for five years and people still walk in and say they live down the street and never knew my store was here."* This is a point of real frustration for small shop owners. We tend to think the whole world should revolve around the world we've created inside our stores. *"I'm here every day and working so hard. How could anyone possibly not know we're here?"*

Just look at yourself and your own busy life. I'll bet there are many businesses in your general area you don't know about either because their message hasn't penetrated your consciousness or because they haven't communicated any messages at all. Maybe they're located on a street you rarely take or a shopping center you don't patronize. If you haven't heard or read about them, if no one told you about them, how would you know they exist? These people simply open their doors every day and expect customers to find them. Are you guilty of the same?

Finally, I hear the very boastful, *"I get all my business through word of mouth."* Word of mouth is a great opportunity for a small business but it isn't enough. By relying solely on others to market for you, without a strategy to push those referrals, you are essentially giving up control. Your job is to drive new business, not sit back and wait for it.

Oh, I wish success was as easy as picking a great location and letting the traffic roll in. And quite frankly, there are certain urban, tourist and mall locations where it *is* pretty easy to attract visitors because these areas provide a steady stream of walk-by or drive-by traffic. But prime locations come with ultra-premium rent rates and aren't suitable for every kind of business.

So let's assume your business, like most, is located in a regular strip, power or lifestyle center, or perhaps an emerging downtown location. Maybe you're on a side street or a less visible location. Perhaps no one can see your sign from the road or construction is blocking access. If you would prefer that your business *not* be the best kept secret on the planet, it's time to work on a comprehensive marketing strategy. And just so you know, dear business owner, a one-time ad placement, a few emails and a Groupon do not a marketing strategy make!

The art of engagement

Engagement. It's my favorite word. Not the "put a ring on it" type of engagement (although who doesn't love a little bling?) but audience engagement. It's that intangible thing that makes people love you and what you do. They're excited, happy and proud to be a part of the experience. An engaged customer loves to spread the word and take credit for discovering you. She encourages everyone else to discover you, too, because it's a reflection of her good taste or judgment. An engaged customer follows you on Facebook and brings friends to your establishment. Sometimes an engaged fan isn't even a customer but "gets" what you're doing and leads others who might benefit right to your door.

An engaged customer is a partner. And the great news about this is you're not paying a dime for the exposure. In fact, you're the one getting paid in sales and new business.

So as you create your marketing strategy, remember the objective is engagement. This is totally opposite of the typical transactional retail mentality that only measures success when the cash register rings. Wrong! The courtship of engaged fans is not just about the sale itself but rather, the cultivation of enthusiasts who will ring the church bells on your behalf.

Where do I begin?

If marketing isn't one of your skill sets, here you'll learn the basic principles of solid grassroots marketing. As a small business, your success will come from cleverness and creativity, not a bigger budget. It will come by creating a community of ambassadors. It will come from intelligence gathering and making smart, fact-based decisions. So whether you decide to take on the marketing yourself or hire professionals, you need to keep focused and curious about alternative solutions combined with solid fundamentals. In this chapter, we'll examine both. We'll look at all the opportunities available to you and how each element can contribute to your success individually - and more importantly - how they can work together to enhance results. From there, you can choose which options you'll incorporate into your overall strategy based on your individual skill level, goals and budget. Remember, you don't need to do it all. You just need to be consistent and powerful using the elements you choose.

Don't even think about money being an obstacle in creating an effective marketing program because, quite frankly, there are dozens of things you can do that cost little or nothing.

Imagine that. You can create the great differentiator for your business for free! It just takes some imagination and if you find yourself falling short in the creative arena, engage friends and family in a fun and productive brainstorming session.

In this module, you also find success stories – and a few failures (hey why make the same mistake twice?) – as well as unique ideas you can begin implementing immediately.

Marketing myths and misunderstandings

Let's start by reviewing some misconceptions and common marketing mistakes.

Believing your store location or shopping center traffic takes the place of marketing

Even stores in the best locations, even the biggest brands need a well-thought out marketing strategy. There is no substitute.

Fear or misunderstanding of the process and potential results

If marketing isn't in your wheelhouse, you may fear you won't do it correctly and ultimately waste time and money. Or you may have unrealistic expectations of what your efforts should produce. Because marketing is measurable, you have the ability to test and experiment until you hit the sweet spot.

Equating lack of results from a particular effort as a failure and then giving up

Getting to success requires tweaking and diligence. Failure doesn't mean stop. It means try something different or new. Sometimes the smallest change can deliver the biggest results. Doing nothing is not an option.

Launching only one strategy

Marketing is a layered effort and you need multiple strategies across different channels.

Using professionals but not directing them correctly or fully understanding their function

If you're going to invest in hiring a pro, it is your job to direct *them*. In order to do that you need to have a clear vision of your goals and a good understanding of how their efforts can get you there.

Out of touch with the competition

As a business owner, you need to know the competition as well as know your own business.

Mass marketing instead of target marketing

Leave the mass marketing to the big guys. Your business will grow small by focusing on hyper-local, hyper-targeted strategies.

You think you know more than you do about marketing

No offense guys, but there are a few of you out there (you know who you are) who are convinced you know everything about marketing your shop. Most of us have a lot to learn and should always be open to that process.

Okay, are you ready to start?

Please follow along with the Marketing Module of the worksheet as you continue reading.

Logo 101

Have you skipped creating a professional logo due to cost? No need to do that anymore. Everyone can have a strong, professional logo thanks to websites like www.99designs.com and www.elance.com through which multiple graphic designers bid for your business. If you don't have a trusted designer in your circle, these types of sites can build your brand identity from logos to signage and packaging design – affordably.

Do you use your logo everywhere and use it properly? Pay attention to proportions and color reproduction quality. If you're printing documents from your computer, there's a good chance the color consistency is going to be off. Be sure to use the right size pixel logo online so that it downloads properly. Never underestimate the power of a strong, well-designed logo as the linchpin of your brand identity.

CHAPTER 10

The Foundation Of Your Plan: Knowing Your Customer

You can't talk to people if you don't know who they are. You can't speak their language if you don't know what's important to them. The key to marketing is to sell prospects what they want, not what *you* think they want. To market effectively, you need to know who is buying from you and why.

We discussed in the MANAGE Module of this book the importance of managing by data. In order to speak in a way that resonates with your customers, you first need to know more about them. Available intelligence through your POS should help lead you to a customer profile, assuming you are asking for, and inputting, the correct information.

When I get the *"everyone's a potential customer,"* line from a client, I know we've got a lot of work to do. You and I both know that even Walmart can't claim that! Your business has a service, product, pricing or personality that's going to appeal more to a certain market segment than others; and sub-segments under that. For example, you might think an upscale men-only hair salon would have an easy target: men. Actually, there will be multiple sub-segments for this business, defined by age, lifestyle, profession, marital status, income and location. You wouldn't deliver the same message to an 18 year old who is into trendy hairstyles as you would a conservative attorney, would you? By collecting and using customer profile information, you no longer need to guess how to market; the answers will be clear as a bell!

Understanding your target customer makes marketing:
- Easier
- More cost effective
- More likely to have a successful outcome

Creating the customer profile

Start with a zip code analysis. Then a gender analysis. Yes, you should be noting if your customers are male or female in your POS because that enables you to further target your marketing and message. In the case of the upscale men's salon, for example, their data showed that women were responsible for nearly 100 percent of gift certificate sales. The marketing message to women would, obviously, be different than that to men.

Next, track age,* average sale and frequency of visit. Then look at your most popular items/services sold. With this information in hand, you'll be able to define your primary customer.

*I don't suggest you ask customers their age but I do recommend you set up an age bracket field in your POS. Instruct your staff to guestimate a customer's age range and tick that box.

It might look something like this: your typical customer is just like Mary (one of your good customers). You know she probably works full time because in speaking with your customers, you've determined anecdotally, the vast majority work outside the home. Mary visits your store 3 times a year and only buys sale items. She spends an average of $200 per visit and lives within two miles of the store. Clearly, she likes your product but is value oriented. With this information you know you have the opportunity to:

1. Find ways to increase the average sale each time Mary visits.
2. Find a different value proposition that will encourage her to buy more frequently.

In the case of a restaurant, you might discover that 60 percent of your customers are regulars, patronizing your business on average, twice per month and spending $40 each time they visit. With this information you know:

1. You have an unhealthy ratio of existing to new customers and you need to focus your marketing on bringing in new clientele.
2. You have an opportunity to increase the average check from your existing customers by implementing an upsell program.

Knowing your customer makes marketing decisions easier, much more targeted and effective.

Customer surveys

If you don't have a POS or haven't been collecting the necessary information to create a customer profile, start collecting it immediately for future use. For the present, there's another way to find out more about your customers – just ask them! Do an online survey (if you have email addresses) or query customers and visitors in store with a simple four question survey. Ask age (by bracket) and zip code. The third question should be customized to your business, i.e. "How would you describe your wardrobe? Work clothes, active wear or weekend wear? Or, "How often to you eat ice cream and what's your favorite flavor?" The fourth question should be one that gives you some insight as to what's important in your customers' lives. You might ask about hobbies or community involvement. Having this type of personal insight enables you to create promotions and programs that resonate with your customers on a deeper level.

Look at your best customers and see what they have in common. Give your target a name and a description, i.e. Mary's Moms and Jean's Teens. It makes it easier to market when you can physically picture that customer as you create your message. You can always plan to reach out to your secondary and tertiary markets but first, go for the low hanging fruit.

Area demographics

When you were negotiating the lease for your store, the leasing agent or landlord may have provided you with professionally compiled area demographics. These reports offer tremendous insight into the makeup of the population base in a 1, 3 and 5 mile radius, showing the neighborhood population breakdown by age, marital status, children living at home, annual income, homeownership, occupation and other categories. Match these demos to your target audience. Is it a good fit?

I worked with a new owner of an existing Italian restaurant. He was planning on changing the concept to more traditional Italian complete with Frank Sinatra music, an old world feel and higher price points. Nice idea, except in examining the area demos, we found the average age in the area was thirty five. It was overwhelmingly populated with young professionals with an average household income of $50,000; hardly the target for the owner's concept. Knowing this prevented him from making an investment in time and money on a concept likely to fail.

BUILDING BLOCK #5
Creating the customer profile
Please complete the answers to these questions on the worksheet.

What information can you access immediately to begin creating your customer profile?

What information do you still need?

How will you gather this data? Via survey? From your POS?

Once you compiled your data, did you find anything that surprised you?

CHAPTER 11

Understanding Your Competition

Your competitors are working hard every day to steal your money. Doesn't it make sense then, to know more about these people with their hands in your pocket? By knowing your competition's strengths and weaknesses and monitoring their strategies, you can proactively adjust your plan to stay ahead of the game.

A 12-year old pizza restaurant's sales were in decline for 3 years running. The owner had not refreshed the store in years and the concept was quite stale. Despite the fact he was selling pizza slices for under $2, he stuck hard to the belief the economy was responsible for his falling revenues. He was so blinded by this belief, he didn't stop to notice that 7 new pizza restaurants had opened within 5 miles of his restaurant! One of his competitors was part of a small chain that was making a huge impact in the market by serving extraordinary coal fired pizza at a price of $20+ per pie, and had a bustling wine and beer business. The recession certainly wasn't a factor *there! The owner never even considered the possibility that it wasn't the economy stealing his money – it was his competitors!*

One of the tricks to properly evaluating competition is understanding there may be a much broader base of businesses vying for your dollar than you think.

Let's say you own a fine jewelry store. Obviously, you should keep tabs on other fine jewelry stores in your area. But it doesn't stop there. Department stores sell fine jewelry, too. Most cities have jewelry exchanges in which someone can set up a small booth at a lower rent and presumably, charge less. Even if you're selling at the highest end, you should track them as well. But the more subtle, underlying competition may not even be in the jewelry category. Since it's a luxury purchase, not a necessity, potential customers can easily opt to spend that money in other ways. They could go on vacation. Buy furniture or clothing. Purchase a designer handbag. Those same dollars can be earmarked for any number of purchases. Understanding that, you realize your competition may be much broader than you anticipated and your marketing efforts need to reflect that.

As CEO of your company, you need to not only be aware of your competitors, you need to be *intimately* aware of them.

I work with four women's boutiques in one shopping center. They are battling each other for market share, yet not one of them followed the other on Facebook. Sure, they'd send "spies" in to look at the merchandise occasionally, but they had absolutely no idea how the others were approaching their social media. Unthinkable! Turns out, one of the boutiques started pulling ahead of the pack by creating a really dynamic Facebook presence and the competition wasn't even aware of it.

Investigate everything about your competition from their window displays to pricing, selection and hours. Visit them on different days and times of day to see if you can get a sense of traffic flow. Review their websites and follow them on social media. Collect any ads they are placing. Track their sales and events. Track the nationals as well. Large companies have access to demographic and trend information you don't, so pay attention to their strategies.

Keep a book or file with this information and analyze it objectively. We tend to focus on what our competition is doing wrong or not as well as us. That's fine. But you also need to be honest about what they're doing that's better or different. Better pricing? Selection? Marketing? Commit to reevaluating this information quarterly so you're always current.

Another tactic for monitoring the competition is staff field trips. Have team members participate in intelligence gathering by sending them out to visit competing stores with a checklist of key items to evaluate. Ask them to deliver their findings at your staff meetings. Lead a discussion about impressions then brainstorm solutions and ideas to move your business ahead of the pack. Field trips are a superior way not just to gather intelligence but to also keep staff engaged and motivated because they are making a contribution to the store's success.

Field trips to best-in-class businesses offer another benefit by giving your employees a firsthand look at what the experience should look and feel like at the highest levels. Let's say you own a fine dining restaurant or a high-end spa or boutique. You may have employees who are trying to deliver an exceptional experience under your guidance, but have not had the benefit of experiencing it themselves! Sending them out into the field will give them a firsthand look at how it should be done. It can be inspirational and transformational.

If you're not keeping up with your competition, there's a good chance you're making decisions based on incorrect assumptions which could cost you time, money and business.

ACTION ITEM #5
Competitive intelligence
Please complete on the worksheet.

Create a plan to gather or organize your competitive intelligence.

Review your findings and determine 3-5 key items your competition is doing well that could potentially impact your business.

Do any items need to be addressed immediately?

CHAPTER 12

Marketing From The Inside Out

You've identified your customers and analyzed the competition. Great job! Now it's time to prepare your store. What happens inside your shop is every bit as much part of the marketing strategy as any advertising or promotion you might do. There's no point in bringing people to your store or restaurant if you're not "dressed up" for the occasion. Every aspect of your store needs to reflect your brand. Let's start with the basics.

Cleanliness

Why bring up cleanliness in a chapter on marketing? Because clean is the start of everything good. Dirt and clutter, on the other hand, make a really bad first impression and could turn off potential customers that visit.

So check those corners for dust bunnies. If you don't have a cleaning service, create a cleaning schedule for your staff and enforce it. Dust, sweep and make sure the bathrooms are clean and are fully stocked. There is NOTHING worse than using a store restroom and finding there's no toilet paper or paper towel. Or how about the mac daddy of sins, a dirty restroom in a restaurant? Makes you wonder what the kitchen is like!

Are your windows and glass doors clean inside and out? I know it sounds so trivial but a door full of fingerprints makes an instant impression on a visitor – and not a good one. Make Windex your new best friend and get scrubbing.

I once worked with a pet store. To say this place was disgusting would be an understatement. There were layers of dirt on every item. The owners kept their own four dogs behind the checkout with pee pads visible to anyone who walked in. Merchandise was, quite literally, thrown onto shelves. Some of the items were so old they were rusted, stained or torn. Even the price tags were yellowed. Quite frankly, I've never seen such an extreme display of filth and disarray. In the midst of it all was a wall of cages filled with high-priced pedigree puppies. It was heartbreaking. All I could think about was how the health of these poor puppies was compromised in this environment.

It was clear the owners had simply given up. Believe it or not, they argued with me, claiming the condition of the store wasn't that bad. They had gotten so sucked into their desperation they stopped looking at things objectively. It took some doing, but I was able to convince them, over time, to begin throwing out, organizing and cleaning. They hauled out truckloads of junk! Unfortunately, this story doesn't have a happy ending. It was too late to save their reputation or their store. They went out of business.

Eliminate clutter. Move those unopened boxes of inventory to the back room. Clean off your front counter! Get rid of anything that gets in the way of you and your customer having a seamless transaction.

Once you're clean and organized, you can begin building your in-store experience.

Sweating the small stuff

Large retailers pay consultants tens and hundreds of thousands of dollars to create the proper ambiance for increased sales. Since you're probably not ready to make that investment, let's dig deep into the details of what makes your store appealing and create a do-it-yourself version.

Lighting

Too bright? Too dark? We've all been in stores and restaurants where the lighting is so dim, you can barely see the merchandise or the food. Or it feels like a fluorescent explosion shining a very harsh and unflattering light on you and those jeans you're trying on.

Lighting is key to setting the proper mood. If you're simply using the overhead lighting supplied by the landlord, it's time to make some changes. A professional lighting plan can be expensive so instead, visit a commercial lighting store with photos and a floorplan of your store. Solicit their advice for track, spot and up lighting solutions that can be easily installed or simply plugged in. If you can, shut the overhead fluorescents off and just use the new lighting. Try adding lamps for charm and character. Is there an opportunity to utilize flameless candles to make it elegant and cozy?

- Test your lighting appeal during the day and night and make adjustments. I see many stores that look good at night but during the day, feel almost depressing.
- Does your lighting allow passersby to see into your store during the day or does it look closed?
- Check for dead spots in the store and use lighting to highlight them.

With a minimal investment you can make a huge transformation with lighting and create a more sales worthy space.

Temperature

Adjust the temperature to be comfortable *for the environment* you are trying to create. If it's freezing, it's hard for a customer to get motivated to try on that little evening dress or order a double scoop of ice cream. I was in a clothing store recently that, for whatever reason, had the temperature in the dressing rooms up to a full tilt broil. I was trying on fall clothes and actually had to stop because it was unbearable. Potential revenue up in smoke!

Is the heat from your ovens sweating out diners sitting close to the kitchen? Move around the different areas of your business and make sure the temperature works to enhance the customer experience.

Music

The best and cheapest way to create ambiance in your store is with music. Armed with a smart phone or a tablet, you can create a disco, a spa or set the stage for romance with the flip of a switch. Music elevates customers' moods and your employees' as well. Remember the earlier story of the coffee shop and how changing their music helped them win back customers? What's the soundtrack for your customer experience?

Phone

Let's talk about your phone policy. *Phone policy? Are you kidding me?* Nope. The phone is as important a portal to your store experience as your front door.

- Do you require employees to answer the phone or are you okay with it going to voicemail?
- Is your voicemail message bright and cheery and reflective of your brand?
- Does the phone caller get priority over the customer standing in front of you?
- Have you trained everyone to answer the phone with a pleasant greeting and speak clearly?
- Is there a protocol for the length of time you will leave a customer on hold? Or the maximum amount of time before you call them back after they leave a message?
- Have you called your store phone when you're not there? It can be enlightening.
- Do you have a special greeting, i.e. *"It's a beautiful day at _____."*?

Lots and lots of questions over a simple phone. Silly? Not in the least. The phone is just another extension of your store experience.

What's your popcorn?

If you tell me you've walked into a movie theater and not been seduced by the aroma of fresh popcorn, I'd say you were lying. That scent is a seductive part of the movie experience. Is there an opportunity to create a memorable scent experience in your store – your own powerful popcorn?

Displays and Merchandising

Display is an art based on science. How you showcase your merchandise makes an instant impression on guests about the quality of your goods. It's the most important physical representation of your brand. Displays set the mood and create delicious anticipation for the prospective buyer.

There are countless psychological studies proving the correlation between store design and purchasing habits. Let's assume they are correct and that the overall layout, look and feel of your store can actually inspire customers to buy. It makes sense.

If you've owned your store for a while, perhaps your merchandising is not current with today's trends. Yes, there was a time when a Mom and Pop store could open up with white slat walls and do okay, but those days are long gone. Today's retail environment is so competitive, it's critical you set the stage for an emotional connection.

By the way, the merchandising discussion is not just targeted to fashion boutiques. Every type of establishment benefits from effective merchandising from dry cleaners and hardware stores to insurance agencies and walk-in clinics.

But I don't have any design talent. While some small shop owners have an affinity for display, many simply wing it. If you can, hire a designer to, at minimum, create a template you can follow or find an interior design student from a local college to assist. If you can't, no worries. It's time to move boldly to a place in which you might not feel entirely comfortable. It's your chance to make a statement that is outrageously you! Put on your creative cap and let's move forward.

Here are some basic fundamentals to get you started.

Avoid overcrowding the store
The more the better! Not so much. So many owners pack their stores from top to bottom, believing the more merchandise on the floor, the more they'll sell. Nothing could be further from the truth. When you overcrowd your racks and shelves, you diminish the perception of the quality of your merchandise and make it difficult for the customer to find what they're looking for or serendipitously discover a treasure.

Put high margin items in high traffic areas and high demand items in low traffic areas
Studies show people are reluctant to go the depth of a retail store so by placing high demand items towards the back, you have the opportunity to entice them with other merchandise while they journey to their final destination.

Display items at different elevations throughout the store to create visual interest. Don't just use racks and shelving. Utilize the walls, the floor, even the ceilings.

Establish a clear line of site from front to back
It's not only good for business, it allows employees to keep an eye on all customers who might be in need of service and helps prevent theft.

I was once asked to do an assessment of a high-end lingerie and linen store with sinking sales. Their ads portrayed a very luxurious, sexy experience. The reality – just the opposite. As I entered the front door, I walked, quite literally, into a wall of towels and sheets thrown into 12" square cubbies that rose nearly up to the ceiling and blocking the line of site to the rest of the store. There were more cubbies along the walls haphazardly filled with merchandise in no particular order. When I got around that maze into the lingerie section, I was faced with rack after rack packed with merchandise and so snugly wedged you could barely walk between them. The racks, rather than being chest height, were extended to about 5' high. And hung from these crowded racks? Hundreds of pairs of granny panties at eye level. Talk about 'in your face.' Not only was their merchandising a disaster, their marketing did not match the realty of the store experience. Imagine a customer who was seduced by the ads only to walk in the store and find the exact opposite. No surprise sales were plummeting.

In another instance, a little girl's beauty spa wanted to increase merchandise sales. They had lots of glitzy t-shirts, pens, tutus, candy and other items little girls love. Unfortunately, they were all displayed at an adult's eye view. We remerchandised at a more kid-friendly height where their mini-clients could see and touch these treasures and influence their Mom's to make a purchase. Merchandise sales went up 240 percent in just 90 days!

Make the most of your prime real estate

Think about what you pay per square foot (PSF) in rent. Every inch of your store should be earning revenue well beyond that actual rental rate, especially when you take into account the non-revenue producing areas like dressing rooms, kitchens, bathrooms and storage rooms. Every piece of your store that's in the public eye has to be productive. As we know, some of these spaces are more sales worthy than others.

The area just to the right of the entrance to your store has been scientifically proven (studies show sixty percent of people will turn right when walking into a store) to be the sweet spot. Create a dynamic display there. As an experiment, calculate the square footage of the display and track the items sold from that area. That number could conceivably be double - or more - of the per square foot sales in other areas of your store. This area is a winner. Try tiered and bundled offers here. By that I mean, buy a hammer and get the nails at a discount. Or buy 3 boxes of nails and get the hammer free. This real estate sweet spot is the perfect place to increase average check by offering the customer an incentive to buy additional product.

I asked a chocolate and candy store owner to create a display in the store's sweet spot. She used a table to feature a bundled offer of five chocolate bars wrapped in a beautiful bow at a price 20 percent lower than if purchased individually. In the first month, they sold 57 bundles versus 27 singles sold the month before. That's 285 chocolate bars, more than 10 times the amount of product!

Is your checkout area producing impulse sales?
We all love to fiddle with items at the checkout counter while we're making our purchases. This is prime impulse buying territory. What's on your counter that customers can't live without?

One boutique had an array of expensive jewelry displayed on their cash wrap. It wasn't selling. We removed the jewelry and replaced it with 3 *bowls of small costume jewelry items at price points under $20. They sold $600 worth in the first week.*

Every place is a marketing opportunity

Are you utilizing dressing and restrooms for marketing? Use signage, photos, posters and even displays in these non-revenue producing areas to promote your brand. You're paying for this square footage so make the most of it.

One store used their dressing rooms to promote a social media contest with signage inviting guests to snap a selfie and post it online for a chance to win a $500 gift certificate. They utilized marketing dead space and boosted their social media presence by capitalizing on the fact they had a captive audience.

Create a mini pop up in your store

Designate an area in your store for a dynamic display that changes regularly. Use themes, interesting displays and cohesive messages to attract visitors. This is a fantastic opportunity to test new products before you commit to a full scale buy.

Display items in ways that make sense to the customer

In addition to being orderly, be sure merchandise is displayed in some sort of cohesive fashion: by color, by size or by usage.

By color

Color is so powerful! People are drawn to their favorite colors even if they're not looking for something specific when they come into your store. Alternatively, using all white or all black in repetition can also make a huge impact.

Typical consignment stores don't focus much on layout and design. My client was no exception. Her store was overcrowded and jammed with merchandise. It was all very unappealing and the owner needed immediate help since she was three months behind in rent. Her location and traffic were good but sales weren't. We removed about 30 percent of the racks, created departments by usage, (tops, dresses, evening, shoes) and displayed all clothes by color. Without spending a nickel, sales began to increase and she was able to catch up on her rent in three months' time.

By usage

Grouping by usage is an excellent way to encourage upselling. It is actually a convenience for the customer to see items that organically belong together. For example:

> Clothing boutique – grouping an entire outfit including jewelry and shoes
>
> Home décor store – grouping coordinated sheets, comforter, curtains and towels
>
> Home improvement store– grouping paint, brushes, painting tape, rollers, cleaning solutions and primer

I work with a magnificent makeup boutique. Their store layout is beautiful with stately makeup stations placed throughout the store. Along the walls, attractive shelving holds skin care, bath and body products grouped by brand. Sales of these products weren't gaining any momentum so we regrouped the merchandise by function (cleansers, toners, eye creams, etc.) with the appropriate signage. Sales of these items rose 24 percent in the first month and nearly 50 percent over the next four months and continue to grow. Don't be afraid to experiment.

Defining your outdoor space

If you have an in-line store in a strip center, it is conceivable people may walk by without even noticing. Owners are usually dismayed and confused by this, but it's a fact. Visitors may be focused on getting to their final destination, talking with their friends or on their cell phones. There may be a glare in your window that prevents them from seeing inside. Perhaps there's no pedestrian level signage to get their attention. Whatever the reason, it's a problem that's easily fixed.

Differentiate yourself from your neighbors by creating a point of visual interest on the outside of your store. If the landlord allows and you have the budget, install an awning or create a more interesting façade. (An awning also helps eliminate glare and allows passersby to easily see into your windows.)

A much cheaper and easier solution is to place a beautiful potted plant on either side of your store. It's inviting and lets visitors know they've entered a defined territory. A sandwich board (a nice one!) can also attract attention. Add balloons for color and excitement.

As a final thought, if your center happens to be dog friendly, simply put out fresh water bowls with a cute little sign. It will give visitors a reason to stop and feel good about your establishment.

Windows

Store windows are a prospect's invitation to your world. Are yours really asking people to come in? Here are some invitation killers:
- Taped signage
- No store identification or hours posted
- Boring window displays

- Sun glare or poor lighting
- Dirty windows

It doesn't matter what type of business you own, your windows are the first line of sight for customers and prospects. Since most stores and restaurants don't have the funds to hire a professional window dresser, here are a few fundamentals and low cost ideas.

First, walk outside and determine the eye level of your store window.
That's your focal point. Is there something at that level that identifies your store name and what you do? An overhead sign is not a substitute for pedestrian level identification.

Create a budget and a schedule for window dressing.
Let's say, for example, you allocate $200 monthly and 4 hours to redress your window and schedule it to be completed on the first Monday of the month after 6 pm, your least busy time. Change your windows, at minimum, monthly.

Explore malls, all types of stores and museums.
Regardless of whether the displays you see cost $100 or $100,000 to create, you will get tons of ideas to inspire you. I take photos everywhere I go and keep them in an inspiration file. You can grab an element from one and a prop from another to create your own exciting windows. The most powerful are generally the simplest with a little flair.

One dry cleaner I know displays large spools of thread in a rainbow of colors organized in rows on shelves in the window. It's quite beautiful and functional as well in that it lets the customer know they also do alterations.

An Italian restaurant had, perhaps, the least expensive and most clever window display I've ever seen. Lined up on shelves in the window were mason jars of tomato sauce. Each jar had a single, large letter on it spelling out the name, MAMA's.

Window Format 101

There are thousands of ways to create a wow factor window. Here's a basic format that works in just about any storefront environment.

Start by crafting a backdrop for your window. A backdrop serves multiple functions. It draws interest, delineates the window area from the rest of the store and it gives your display a pop of color for additional visual appeal.

Craft your backdrop out of fabric, colored photography paper, colored foam board, see-through mesh, an extra-large chalkboard or even a bed sheet. Simply attach your backdrop from wires or a rod attached to the ceiling. Once you install the wire, you can easily change the material with very little time or money. If you're feeling a bit more adventurous, print the backdrop with a photo or graphic that enhances your theme (a photo of the beach for summer clothing, a couple having fun painting their living room for a DIY hardware store promotion). Or you can use a printed backdrop to advertise a promotion. For example, if you're having a big annual sale, print the word "Sale" large as life on the background. This single word creates a high impact visual that effectively delivers your message and can be reused each time you have a sale.

Regardless of how simple or intricate a backdrop, it will give your windows personality, color and create a great foundation for your creative inspiration. Now it's time to decorate.

Take full advantage of the three dimensional aspects of a window display
Clothing stores are often guilty of the "3 maids in a row" syndrome – putting 3 mannequins in line, side-by-side. So boring! The eye reacts more favorably to displays at different elevations and depths within the window.

Use interesting objects to create elevation
Try boxes, crates, stacks of books, paint cans, dishes, even chairs as display bases. A quick trip around your garage or the flea market should produce some interesting choices.

Create a "ceiling"
Hang individual elements on wire from the ceiling. Whether they're crystals, paint brushes or Christmas ornaments, hanging objects or stringing lights from above easily creates dimension.

Create a floor
Use the base of the display to further enhance your window. Paint it (maybe stripes?), lay tile or carpet or drape it with fabric. Any type of material or texture that compliments your theme will work. I saw a gorgeous store window in Paris in which they built a white plexi floor. In that floor, they drilled holes that held little glass vases in rows, each filled with a fresh bud. That may be a bit too much maintenance but you can certainly adapt that idea by using fake flowers in small vases or line paint can lids (color side up) to create a similar effect.

Choose a theme

Maximize your hard work by creating a theme and integrating it throughout your shop and in your marketing. Think beyond the traditional four season change and how you can inject some individual store personality.

I saw a clever window display for a store holding their annual sale. They covered large laundry detergent boxes with the word "Sale" and stacked them in the background. They used cotton laid throughout the window to emulate soap suds. A great idea for continuing this theme would be to create a tag line, i.e. "Clean up at our annual sale" and use that theme in ads, on the website, in social media and email marketing. By tying this clever idea across all marketing channels, you increase its impact exponentially.

Signage

In my opinion, there's one category of business that does signage right-parking garages. Think about it. Parking garages generally have 2 large signs:

PARKING

ENTER HERE

That's everything you need to know. They get their message out loud and clear and if you're looking for a place to park, there is no mistaking the fact that this is where you need to be. Most store signage, however, isn't that clear. In fact, I would say signage is the biggest missed opportunity in retail.

First things first, take down every handwritten and random computer generated sign taped to a door, window or wall. No tape! As an alternative, purchase inexpensive Lucite sign holders, frames, easels or clear suction cups to display signs.

Just about any Microsoft program (Word, PowerPoint, Publisher) offers free design templates. Create an entire program using the same template and the same fonts. Use different size signage for different displays and messages but always use the same basic method of display. If you decide to place your signs in silver frames, use silver frames throughout.

Create signage for:

- Sales and specials
- Brand messages
- Point of sale and shelf talkers with details about featured items
- Department identification and directional signage
- Store policies
- Menu of services
- Social media and email signup requests
- Upselling or special offers
- Complimentary services (delivery, gift wrap)
- Lifestyle graphics – show your product in use (your vendors may be able to provide these at no cost)

Signage makes it easy for a customer to find what they want, learn what you have, order and check out. I work with so many owners who will tell me about all the great perks and services available and, in looking around, see absolutely no evidence of them. *"My staff will tell customers about them."* Not good enough guys. You need to shout it out at every possible opportunity.

Service businesses and merchandising

Good merchandising applies to service businesses, too. Whether you have an insurance or real estate agency, a medical office or travel agency, your in-store experience is just as important. If your waiting area is dull and furnished with out-of-date chairs and old carpet, it's time for a makeover. A coat of paint, new lighting, a few new chairs and some artwork can change the perception of everyone who walks in your door. (We redid a podiatrist's office with beautiful black and white photos of feet. Spectacular!) The waiting area is also a terrific place for soft sales of products related to your business for an additional revenue stream.

A travel agency client had an office that was amazingly cluttered and – gray! Visitors were greeted by faded walls, gray cubicles and piles of paper everywhere. There was no real lobby or seating area and no brochures displayed. One would never know they were selling high-end cruises and their job was to transport people to faraway lands around the world. After creating a better paperwork system to improve productivity and eliminate clutter, we set about recreating the office. Over the course of a weekend, the owners painted the office a beautiful sea blue, created a small seating area filled with gorgeous, colorful travel brochures provided by the cruise lines, added a few plants, and voila, an office that represented the company's brand and quality.

Take a critical look at your store inside and out. What can you do to make it more inviting or exciting? It's time to work some magic!

ACTION ITEM #6
Your Store
Answer these questions on the worksheet

Does your store need improvement in the following areas?
 Cleanliness
 Lighting
 Temperature
 Music
 Scent/Aroma
 Phone

Displays and Merchandising
Evaluate your store for the following:
 I have a merchandise display strategy and adhere to it
 Store aisles are easy to navigate
 Merchandise is easy to find and clearly labeled
 High margin items are located in high traffic areas/ high demand items in low traffic areas
 There is a clear line of site from front to back
 Merchandise is attractively displayed at various elevations throughout the store
 Store has an effective display in a prime real estate area that changes regularly
 There is a display of impulse items at the checkout and I am tracking those sales
 I am using dead areas for store marketing (dressing rooms, rest rooms, lobbies, etc.)
 I change my windows often with interesting and effective displays

My outdoor space is well defined and attracts attention
at a pedestrian eye level

My in-store signage is consistent, attractive and
represents my brand

List any other improvements needed in your store:

CHAPTER 13

Sorting Out The Online Marketing Toolbox

The good news is, today's independent business has a vast array of online marketing tools available to them. The bad news is, today's independent business has a vast array of online marketing tools available to them. What should be an exciting smorgasbord of opportunities can turn into an indigestible blur. You probably have countless sales reps at your door each week trying to sell you iPad loyalty programs. You read every day in the news about businesses creating an overnight success simply using free social media. There are companies offering to create your website for thousands or even tens of thousands of dollars and ads promoting do-it-yourself versions for free. And what do you do about online reviews? It's an awful lot to process.

What are the best options? Where should you start? I suggest you put off making any decisions involving online marketing until you learn about all the tools available and how they work. Then, and only then, will you be in a position to make an informed decision. So let's go.

Tech 101

It's time to have a little chat about online marketing. If you're not a fan, I'll bet your eyes just rolled back into your head. Before you turn the page, give me a second to explain my take.

We're all good at certain things and there's a really good chance that you, like me, cannot build your own website or find posting daily on Facebook an annoyance. We've all had our "throw the computer against the wall" moments. But today, like it or not, technology runs our businesses and drives our marketing. We're all well-served by overcoming our fears and embracing what technology offers us –an inexpensive way to gain amazing exposure and the competitive edge necessary to grow small.

Here's another piece of amazing news! Most online platforms provide free analytics, enabling you to measure results in real time! Think about that. You can immediately know if your efforts are resonating with customers, giving you the opportunity to expand successful strategies and tweak those that aren't working as well. (More about this in the MEASURE module.)

One of the biggest reasons business owners become paralyzed in the face of technology is the sheer volume of options. *"How can I possibly manage my website, Facebook, Twitter, Instagram, LinkedIn, Pinterest and whatever social media du jour that might pop up tomorrow?"* The good news is, you don't have to manage them all. In addition to your website, choose one or two social media outlets and focus on making your presence on them count! Your target customer will help determine which are best for you.

In this chapter, you'll learn about the various platforms and most importantly, what each does to enhance your business. We'll cover the most commonly asked questions and deal with the issues I have found to be consistent among small retailers and restaurant owners.

Even if you're comfortable navigating these tools, it's important to understand how all the pieces work together to maximize their benefits. You have to know what something's supposed to do in order to manage it correctly, right?

Experiment

Let's start with a little experiment. First, do a Google (or whatever browser you prefer) search of your business category and city, for example, pet stores, Dallas. If your website, Facebook page, Yelp, Google or other reviews aren't coming up on the first page or two of the results, your technology isn't working for you.

Next, Google your business name. Are there multiple results, including your website (potentially different pages displayed?), Facebook page and links to review sites? If there is little mention of your establishment, again, your technology strategy isn't working for you.

Remember, 90 percent of people begin their search for a local business online.* If you're not visible, you're not even part of the decision.
*ZMOT

So before we start the discussion about how to create your strategy, let's take a look at how your online efforts contribute to your search rankings with some basic, behind the screen information.

Organic Search and Search Engine Optimization (SEO) for non-techies

There are people out there who actually understand how this stuff works. I am not among them. If I put in keywords (pet stores, Dallas) what dictates what appears and what doesn't in the search results? What the hell is organic search?

In brief, organic search is how the Google gods figure out what to display based on a keyword search. Their little robots "crawl" all existing online content and the businesses or people with the most/newest/relevant content generally get higher rankings. *(There are actually 200 components to the Google ranking algorithms including domain age, keyword usage and even grammar and spelling. Most of these components should be addressed in the web development stage.)* Online content includes your website, social media postings, blogs and online reviews. Google rewards changing and new content with better search rankings so the more interaction on your Facebook page, the more you add content to your website, the more reviews you get – the better your organic search results. Simple enough? Remember our stat about 90 percent of people beginning their search for a local business online? That's reason enough to get your online presence in order.

So the lesson here is that one of the ways to get all the great search benefits of your online presence is to continually update your content. Unfortunately, way too many small businesses create websites when they open their doors and rarely touch them again, or go days and weeks without posting on social media. This type of neglect not only prevents you from delivering your message, it can actually render your online presence useless. So when we discuss marketing through technology, it's important to understand you can't just "set it and forget it." To get the results you want you have to work it.

Search Engine Optimization (SEO) is the technique used to properly configure a website for enhanced organic search results. It primarily involves creating/editing content and coding to increase the site's relevance, and ultimately, it's ranking in organic search. As mentioned earlier, effective SEO starts in the web development stage. Yes, there are certainly things you can do to increase the chance your site will show up in a search as explained in the organic search section above. If you continue to change your content, use strategic keywords and pay attention to your social media posts and reviews, you may be able to get by without the expenditure of hiring an SEO professional.

Another effective SEO tactic is backlinking – links from other websites directed back to yours. You might work with your neighboring stores to cross promote each other's website with backlinks. You generally see this on a Partners or Neighbors page on a website. It's a simple, free way to help improve search rankings.

Depending on the type of business you own, you may have to budget to optimize your site. Pizza restaurants, because of the vast amount of competition, need to have high ranking websites. Personal trainers, doctors and restaurants are best served by an investment in SEO as well. Do some thoughtful web browsing for the competition in your area and decide whether or not this should be part of your marketing budget.

Dynamic Content/ Content Management Systems

We know we have to provide new content in order to get better search results. Changing content is referred to as dynamic content. According to a study cited on Entreprenuer.com, content marketing costs 62 percent less than traditional marketing and generates about three times as many leads. What more powerful evidence do you need to pay attention to your content?

You can pay a professional to update your website or you can ask your web developer to build your site with a content management system (CMS) which gives you the ability to easily add copy and photos yourself –a much cheaper and more flexible alternative. Most content management systems operate much the same as your basic Microsoft Office software so with a little training, you can be the master of your own domain- literally.

CHAPTER 14

The Online Tools

The online toolbox is vast. Here is an overview of the key platforms to consider for your retail establishment.

Your Website

Here's what you need to know in a nutshell:

You MUST have a website

A website is the primary tool for helping people find and learn more about your business. It is the hub of today's marketing strategy. It's the handshake. The introduction. The, "welcome to our home" portal for new and existing customers. It should be a truly accurate representation of your business in cyberspace.

A webpage is not a website

Simply putting your name, hours and a business overview on the Internet will not help potential customers find you or for that matter, get to know your brand.

Your website needs to look good and read well

Your online presence must be a visually appealing reflection of your brand. Don't skimp on the graphics. Good quality photos and artwork can elevate your website from bland to bold. If you don't have original photography, consider using professional shots provided by vendors or purchase stock photos. (Stock photos are professional shots that can be downloaded and used, generally, for just a few dollars. Check out sites like istockphoto.com and shutterstock.com.) Quality photography is especially important for any establishment selling food. Unless you are very good at lighting and food styling, you might end up posting unappetizing photos that can actually turn people off rather than entice them to visit.

Keep copy short and powerful, at least on the primary pages. If you need to go in-depth on a particular topic, provide a link to the full version on interior pages.

Use a minimum number of type fonts, sizes and colors throughout the site. If your web designer hasn't set up a style sheet, you can simply decide for yourself that headlines will all be the same font and size. The same goes for body copy and other features so there is a consistent look throughout the site.

Functionality and content

At minimum, your website should have the following functionalities and content in order to best serve as a business tool:

Home page navigation

Use a maximum of 4 or 5 navigation buttons. Think about how a visitor will use the site and be sure they can easily find their way to various pages - and back again.

Email capture

This call to action should be front and center on your home page. One of the most common mistakes I see is the request for an email address buried on an interior page. Give your visitors a visible place – and a reason – to submit their email addresses so you can continue to communicate with them. You can offer a discount coupon, a free monthly newsletter or the opportunity to enter a contest in exchange for an email submission.

Brand message

Keep it short and sweet but let your visitors know what makes you special.

Social media icons with links

Make it easy for people to follow you by letting them click right through to your social media pages.

Address, phone and hours
Put all pertinent information on the home page. Don't discourage potential customers from communicating by hiding your phone number. Further, be sure you're responsive to communication generated from your website.

Representative photos of merchandise and your store
Change these often and tag them with keywords to assist with your optimization.

Testimonials and reviews
You have clients who love you. Let the world know.

Additional content

About you and your store
What's the backstory behind your business? Does your bakery use a recipe from your Dutch grandmother? Say so! Customers love real stories and any opportunity to make your business personal will further endear people to your brand.

Menu of services
Provide a complete list of products and services, including complimentary offerings like delivery.

Staff credibility
Service businesses (insurance agencies, medical providers) and personal service providers (salons, spas,

personal trainers) are well-served by introducing their staff members and flaunting credentials.

Online ordering or appointment setting
Not to be confused with ecommerce, this functionality allows customers to make appointments or order lunch without picking up the phone. It's a tremendous convenience and becoming more and more mainstream.

These are the basics of a solid website. From here, you can add customized content and features to make your site more interesting and best reflect your business.

Whether you're just building your site or doing a refresh, you need to fully understand how you'd like your website to function.

What do you want people to do when they get there?
How often would you like them to come back?
Is the purpose to provide information? Sell? Build credibility?

Answer these questions before you begin work on your website in order to create an effective and fully functioning tool.

Mobile apps vs. mobile responsive design
Do I need an app? Almost every client asks this question and the answer is almost always "No." A mobile app provides a propriety service or convenience delivered via a smartphone or tablet. For example, you use your bank's mobile app to check your balance or transfer money from anywhere. Their apps makes it easier for you

to do business with them. Unless you can offer an opportunity to purchase or communicate that has potential for widespread use, an app is probably not worth the thousands you'd have to invest. There are other free and low charge options for developing simple apps. Checkout sites like www.como.com where can you build a simple app yourself at no charge.

A better option is to work with your web designer to create a mobile responsive design for your website. This simply means your website adapts to the size of the screen on which it is displayed. So whether the visitor is accessing it on a smart phone, a tablet, a laptop or a desktop, they will all have an optimal viewing experience. Since more and more people are connecting through smartphone and tablets, your website should function properly across all platforms.

ACTION ITEM 7
Your Website
Evaluate your website on the worksheet.
> Easy to navigate
> Adding/changing content on a regular basis
> Major functionalities available and working
> All links working – no errors
> Brand message conveyed clearly via copy and photos

Social Media

It's free! Lots of people use it! It's available to everyone. What could be better? If you aren't using social media to grow small, you're missing one of the greatest competitive advantages of all time! For some of you, social media's accessibility and lack of fees will make it the foundation of your marketing program. So decide which one (or two) are best for you, understand their purpose and go for it.

Social media platforms include:
Facebook
Twitter
Google+
You Tube
LinkedIn
Blogging
Pinterest
Instagram
Foursquare
Social Media
Review sites (i.e. Yelp)
Short form video (i.e Vine)
Social bookmarking (i.e. StumbleUpon and Reddit)
Forums
Snapchat
Podcasting

Like any tool, free or not, social media requires a strategy, a goal and a commitment. Some owners hand off social media posting duties to young employees (*they know about that stuff*) and walk away. Not good. If you're going to make it part of your plan, you need to work it properly to get an appropriate return. The better it performs for your business, the more motivated you'll be to keep going.

If you need a tutorial on the basics of social media, the internet is overflowing with information about the do's and the don'ts, basic setup information, strategy ideas and case studies. YouTube offers a multitude of "how-to" videos. There are countless experts offering free webinars. There's really no excuse not to be in the know. A little research and you'll be a pro, or at the very least, armed with enough knowledge to direct someone thoughtfully.

Why you need to integrate social media into your marketing strategy

Thanks to their explosive popularity, social media platforms are causing marketing mania. According to the 2014 Social Media Marketing Industry survey of marketing executives published by the Social Media Examiner:

- More than half (59%) of respondents used social media to attract consumers
- 99% consider social media important for their businesses
- Facebook (94%) and Twitter (83%) were the two most popular platforms followed by LinkedIn (71%) and YouTube (57%)
- Respondents cite the top benefits of social media marketing as increased exposure and traffic
- 66% use social media for lead generation
- 61% use social media to improve search rankings

The study also cites that Facebook dominates in the business-to-consumer space and is the number one choice of marketers.

Using social media really isn't an option anymore. The benefits – and the fact your competition is probably posting as we speak– demand you engage.

Hashtag marketing

We've all seen them and some of them are darn clever. But what do hashtags really mean and how do they enhance your marketing? Hashtags are simply words or phrases that tie posts together by topic for search purposes. One of the most popular hashtags, #throwbackthursday, organizes posts of old photos using that hashtag. A hashtag might be a phrase (#maytheforcebewithyou), a description (#littleblackdress), a person (#santaclaus), an emotion (#chocolatemakesmehappy), the name of your shopping center or an event. For example, #raceforthecure or #getyourpinkon will lead you to posts about various Susan G. Komen events.

Hashtags started on Twitter and are now used on most social media platforms, including most recently, Facebook.

So let's say your business is having a fundraiser during October, Breast Cancer Awareness Month to benefit breast cancer research. You can include the #raceforthecure or #getyourpinkon hashtags and your posts will become part of the larger conversation by others interested in the cause, not just your followers. Pretty simple, right?

You are free to create any hashtag you'd like to start your own following but there are a few do's and don'ts.

Research hashtags before you choose one

The seemingly perfect hashtag may already be in use for something totally unrelated or inappropriate.

Keep hashtags short and memorable

Use the same hashtag(s) across all your social media posts

Best practices advise not using more than two hashtags in a post. A study by Buddy Media shows that:

> Tweets with hashtags receive two times more engagement than a Tweet without one.

Tweets with one or two hashtags have a 21 percent higher engagement than those with three or more hashtags.

The four B's of Social Media

Be Authentic
Let your personality shine on social media. If you're quick witted or clever, caring and nurturing, a born teacher or a social activist, use that personality to engage your social media audience.

Be Present
Post on a consistent schedule. You can't be in one day and out the next. Your fans and followers need to know you're as committed to the platform as they are. You also need to be responsive. Thank new followers. Ask them questions. Reward their dedication.

Be Prepared: The Potential Backlash
People are free to post whatever they like. Usually it's a question, a comment or a compliment. Sometimes, it's not so nice. A disgruntled customer can really set your universe on its ear – even if the negative comments are unfounded. Understand that at some point, this is going to happen to you and it won't be fun.

Have a policy prepared as to how you are going to handle this type of disruption. Address the problem quickly – and publicly – online. If the customer still isn't satisfied, try to take the conversation off line via private messaging, phone or email. The objective isn't to be right; it's to let your followers know you're aware of the issue. If the vitriol spreads and encourages multiple negative comments, you need to examine the legitimacy of the problem, resolve it on your end and make a public announcement as to how you solved it. Act quickly and decisively.

Be Creative

Consider your social media posting as entertainment, it's not all about selling. Delight your fans and followers with interesting posts and photos that make them think, make them feel good, make them laugh or teach them something new. Solicit their opinion. By doing this, you make them appreciate your brand even more.

A recent episode of Shark Tank (no surprise this is my favorite TV show) featured a young couple who began an online women's clothing website (nothing new there, right?) and grew it into an $8 million dollar business in just four years. That got the Sharks' attention! Their brand differentiator was providing a curated and frequently updated selection of clothing and accessories under fifty dollars. The owner would go to the clothing markets weekly and posted items on social media to get opinions about merchandise from followers. Instead of guessing what to buy, she involved potential customers in the decision making, not only engaging them but giving them exactly the products they wanted. Brilliant!

Another great example of social media creativity is from a jump rope fitness company in New York. They teach fitness classes centered around jumping rope and sell related products. To insure everyone has a great time while sweating through the double unders, the company creates new class themes each week set to music. They grew their Facebook presence by asking fans to select music for the next week's class. They would post something like, "We're looking for song recommendations for next week's Octoberfest class." By doing that, they were able to engage followers in the conversation and make them part of the decision. They would then post the final playlist along with a, usually, humorous photo to further promote the theme. That strategy, along with some well-placed how-to videos, class announcements and a sprinkling of products for sale, helped them boost their business into an international success.

The platforms
For the purposes of our discussion, we're going to talk about the most popular and relevant social media platforms.

Facebook
This mac daddy social media platform still reigns as the top performer in sheer numbers (over a billion active users) and offers a broad audience of all ages. The singular goal of a Facebook presence is to create a dialogue with customers and fans. Posts need to be compelling to gain interest and encourage likes, shares and comments.

Each time you post something that causes one of your fans to like a post, that post then shows on that fan's page for all their friends to see, giving you more visibility. Those friends of fans may then choose to share the post or follow you as well, increasing your exposure exponentially. As discussed earlier, an active Facebook page can also significantly improve your organic search results.

You may have heard rumblings about Facebook Edge Rank, a system that only feeds your posts to certain fans. Before Edge Rank, every post would appear to every follower. Now, due to sheer volume, Facebook uses an algorithm to limit the number of feeds. While this is extremely annoying, it makes compelling content even more important since fan interaction is one of the keys to increasing their chance of receiving your posts. In addition, be aware that recently introduced algorithms also discourage strictly promotional content.

Tips for using Facebook to Grow Small

Make Facebook part of the customer experience

Put a sign on your cash wrap inviting customers to like you on Facebook. Offer a small discount or gift if they use their smartphone to do it on the spot or place an iPad at the checkout for this purpose.

If you are really trying to build your fan base, ask your current fans for help. Have a "like us on Facebook week" or run a contest to help increase likes and shares. Share an end goal, keep your followers updated on progress and celebrate with them when it's achieved.

Track the types of posts that are getting the most engagement and look for patterns so you can tweak future posts to get the maximum benefits.

For important announcements, you can pin a single post to the top of your Facebook page. Create your post and after it appears on the page, hover over the right hand corner which will reveal the pin prompt. Pin posts to highlight new merchandise, a sale or an event. Pins expire in seven days.

Promote an event

Under the settings section on your Facebook page, look for Apps. Here you will find an event app that allows you invite fans to an event and even receive RSVP's. You can post updates and message fans about the event, post photos and respond to posts. It's free!

Paid promotion

Facebook offers the opportunity to boost the exposure of a post, run ads, or promote your website at a very reasonable price – as little as $5 per day for the length of time and total budget you choose. You can select the makeup of the audience that will be served these posts or ads by gender, location and interests. You can even choose to serve them inside or outside of your existing fan base. For a $5 daily post boost, Facebook claims you'll receive 4-17 likes.

Twitter

With 271 million active users, Twitter has created a bustling community of people and businesses making an impact in 140 characters or less.

According to Twitter:

- 74% of people who follow small and medium-sized businesses follow to get updates on future products.
- 47% of people who follow brands on Twitter are more likely to visit that company's website.
- 72% of followers are more likely to make a future purchase.

The platform recently introduced several new services including:

"While you were away," a feature that highlights important tweets posted since your last visit.

The ability to shoot, edit and post videos directly through Twitter.

Private group messaging.

Cupcake Store Creates Sweet Success on Facebook

Can social media really produce results for a small business? Here's a case study that says resoundingly, "Yes!" A struggling cupcake store client had virtually no Facebook presence. They had a paltry 398 followers after three years in business, limited postings and little fan engagement. We developed a three-prong Facebook strategy:

1. Regular postings of products (photos of yummy looking cupcakes, cookies, coffee, tea, and specials) and promotion of newly-created birthday party packages for kids.

2. Development and promotion of cupcake decorating classes. Posts generated interest thanks to photos of the irresistible final product attendees would be creating in class. After the class, we posted photos of attendees enjoying the experience.

3. Creation of a Test Kitchen concept. The owners of this business are a husband and wife team. The husband loves being in the kitchen and creating new baked delicacies. We used that passion as their brand differentiator to create the Test Kitchen. The concept was simply that twice each month, on a Wednesday, the

   husband would go into the kitchen and create something new. They would post pictures of him in the kitchen, covered with flour or elbow deep in batter to provoke curiosity. The following day, Thursday, was Test Kitchen day. Anyone who visited the store would be given a free Test Kitchen card (10 Test Kitchen visits got you a $5 gift certificate. Emails were required to receive the card, shoring up their database) and a free sample of the new concoction. Visitors were then asked to rate the new product as a Flip (Flip your lid over it) or a Flop. The owners posted the results on Friday. They were totally honest about customer reaction – even if it wasn't great. It was totally authentic and people loved it!

Results

Over the course of just 30 days:

1. They posted a coconut macaroon special that was seen by someone who ordered 8000 coconut cookies – a huge order for a store that size.

2. Follower base grew from 398 to 600 (within months it grew to 1250).

3. Engagement from fans grew as high as over 100 likes for certain posts.

4. They began booking birthday parties, posting photos and "mom" testimonials which generated even more bookings.

5. Decorating classes began filling to capacity, adding yet another revenue stream and creating a whole new loyal fan base.

Total cost: $0

Twitter is easy to set up and use. What's more, you can set up your Twitter account to automatically feed to your Facebook page so it's doing double duty!

Tips for using Twitter to Grow Small

Start with a stunning graphic and an intriguing description. "Women's clothing store" might be accurate, but "We dress the women everybody's staring at" is a bit more interesting. Be sure to let people know what you do and emphasize your branding.

Size your logo or profile graphic appropriately. Your profile graphic accompanies every Tweet and shows up really small, especially on smartphones. You may want to consider a logo modification just for this purpose. For example, *The New York Times* just uses its logotype "T" on Twitter.

Strategically choose people and businesses to follow. There's a good chance they will, in turn, follow you as a courtesy. Choose influencers in your community, potential customers, and, of course, customers.

Be sure to thank them for following you and comment on their Tweets.

Twitter moves fast so don't be afraid to post multiple times during a day. Just be sure to space your Tweets out during different day parts.

Ask your employees to retweet your postings to attract their followers as well.

Use hashtags and photos/graphics to enhance your Twitter posts.

Create a Twitter landing page on your website. Rather than just bringing Twitter followers to your website home page, create a landing page just for them that introduces new acquaintances to your business. It's a nice way of letting them know you appreciate their Twitter support. This page can also host Twitter follower-only specials.

Don't just Tweet randomly. Tweeting for business is not about stream of consciousness thoughts. Develop a strategy around your content by creating a list of topics that will be of interest to your audience and relevant to your business and use that list as a guideline for your Tweets.

Instagram

Instagram is the new kid on the block with a mission to "capture and share the world's moments." During the writing of this book, Instagram exceeded 300 million users making it larger than Twitter. Should your business use Instagram? The answer is yes if it's a highly visual business that appeals to an 18-34 year old, primarily female audience.

Like Twitter, Instagram is hashtag driven. Its unique offering is a tool to filter photos to give them a distinctive look. Instagram also supports video.

Instagram is a natural for fashion, travel, food and other visually interesting businesses. But let's think outside the Instagram box and see where it might drive exposure for a commodity business. Take a dry cleaner for example. One doesn't generally think of a dry cleaner as having a brand or personality, but they might create one by posting photos of staff happily cleaning and mending your clothes under the hashtag #cleanandhappy or tracking a #dayinthelife of a beloved piece of clothing.

If you're in a category of business that doesn't have a lot of Instagram competition, it might be worth seeing how you can use the platform to differentiate your brand.

Tips for using Instagram to Grow Small

The key to Instagram is to utilize authentic, fun and interesting photos – not necessarily professional or contrived, but high quality and with lots of pizzazz.

Use brief messages and hashtags. Instagram recommends no more than three.

Begin your Instagram campaign by first following others, liking their posts and commenting.

Tag others to help grow your exposure.

Don't post URLs. Users can't click links on Instagram.

YouTube

While the other social media platforms get lots of buzz about their usefulness as business tools, video may just be pulling ahead of the pack.

According to the 2014 Social Media Industry Report, video is the number two medium marketers are interested in exploring for 2015. Nearly 3 in 4 surveyed plan to increase their use of original video. Why? Because it's proving to be an extremely effective marketing tool. It communicates information quickly and is often more exciting than the written word. When consumers are interested, they listen. The more they listen, the more they're compelled to take action.

In the past, small businesses shied away from video due to the expense of professional shooting and editing. Today, people are creating short, interesting, informative and entertaining clips shot with inexpensive video cameras, even smart phones or tablets.

People love video. According to YouTube, people watch, on average, over 20 hours of on-line video per month. We're watching movie trailers, cute babies, stupid people and grumpy cats. But we're also doing business and building brands. In fact, studies show 52 percent of consumers are more confident in a product after watching a video online. Further, putting video on your website makes it 53 times more likely that you'll land on the first page of Google search results. That's got to peak your interest!

Video "lives" on YouTube so you merely need to sign up to start your own free channel and upload your creation. Done.

Tips for using YouTube to Grow Small

- Customize your channel with your logo, colors and brand message.
- Keep on shooting! Post videos on a regular schedule.
- Request users subscribe to your channel so they'll be notified when new videos are posted.
- Title your videos thoughtfully, choosing the right category and tags, keeping keyword search in mind.
- Write a great description of your video to inspire visitors to click and view.
- Respond to comments.
- Once you post your video to YouTube you can link it to your website or other social media platforms.

Pinterest

Another rising social media star, Pinterest usage is, according to a 2012-2013 Pew research study, growing faster than any other social media platform. Pinterest is about women (they account for 80 percent of its users) and is being utilized by business categories with the broadest appeal to that market: fashion, home décor, crafts, wedding and travel. What began as a recreational site, Pinterest is getting more aggressive about its role in business. For retailers, it's an opportunity to improve search engine optimization and drive traffic to your website. If these goals align with your strategy and your market is women, you may want to consider Pinterest.

To use Pinterest, create an account and begin posting your own captioned photos or videos and pinning others' posts to your boards. When users begin searching for posts on a specific topic, let's say honeymoons, your post will show up in the search. Similar to a Facebook share, users "pin" their favorite posts to their own boards which are, in turn, seen by their followers. The exponential exposure for your business works the same as with any other social media.

Tips for using Pinterest to Grow Small

The rules are essentially the same for Pinterest as other social media:

- Create a Pinterest business, not personal, account.
- Post an interesting profile about your business.
- Use provocative descriptions for your posts but keep them short with a focus on keywords that will help visitors find your products.
- Start by following other people, perhaps your vendors, local influencers, national influencers in your industry and your customers. (By following customers, you'll gain insight into their personal style preferences which may help in better serving them. It's like free research!)
- Pinterest is dependent on interesting and high quality images to attract attention. Interestingly, images without faces are repinned 23 percent more often.
- Use hashtags to categorize your pins.
- Create different boards for specific audiences, for example, a candy store might have a board focused on corporate gifts.
- Best practices suggest pinning daily, later in the afternoon and after 8 pm when women are typically doing their recreational computer surfing.
- Include links to your website on your pins. That way, when pins are shared they create backlinks to your site which could help improve your site's search ranking.

A few words about LinkedIn

LinkedIn is primarily a business-to-business tool. As the CEO of your company, you may find it a valuable place to make connections, learn and build your own personal brand.

There are thousands of groups on LinkedIn you can join for free. You may find groups that share information about retail operations, focus on your specific type of retail (i.e. liquor stores) or even groups of local retailers in your area. Finally, you might find LinkedIn useful for recruiting staff, especially if your needs require someone with specialized experience.

Create your profile and invite your vendors to connect with you. Ask other business people to recommend you using the endorsement tool. LinkedIn is an excellent platform for establishing your credibility as a business person which may come in handy when applying for a loan or negotiating a new vendor contract or lease.

Blogs

We'll wrap up our discussion on social media with blogging. A blog is a fantastic way to add dynamic content to your website and improve SEO. It's also an opportunity to engage your audience with more detailed information than you can provide through other social media outlets.

You don't have to be a great writer to have an effective blog. A few paragraphs from the heart – speaking to the personality of your business – and thoughtfully selected photos can help you start a new communication channel. Blogs are especially effective for demonstration and education (a boutique may blog about styling, a craft store may use their blog to show how to knit a sweater). This type of content has great perceived value to a prospect or customer and keeps your business upfront and relevant.

The what/when/how of posting

What kind of content can I write or post? How can I think of something every day? When's the best time to post? Am I posting too much? Too little? Here are research findings to answer some of your questions.

Facebook facts:

- Content posted later in the day gets more likes and shares.*
- Peak posting time for likes and shares is 8:00 pm.*
- Peak share time is 6:00 pm.*
- 33% of Facebook postings are mobile.*
- Asking fans to share results in a share rate 7 times higher. **
- Asking fans to comment results in a 3.3 times higher comment rate.**
- Asking fans to like a post results in a 3 times higher like rate.**
- Posts with 80 characters or less receive a 23% higher interaction rate that longer posts. **
- Photo posts receive interaction rates 39% higher than average. **
- Posts that ask a question at the end have a 13% higher interaction rate than those with a question in the middle and a 2 times higher comment rate. **
- Using a "fill in the blank" question to query fans results receive 4 times as many comments **
- The average Facebook post has a lifespan of 3 hours.***

Twitter facts
- Optimal time of the day to get Retweets is 5:00 pm.*
- Twitter engagement rates for brands are 17% higher on Saturday and Sunday. **
- Tweets posted between 8 am and 7 pm get a 30% higher interaction rate.**
- Tweets with image links have engagement rates 2 times higher than those without.**
- Tweets that ask for Retweets receive a 12 time higher retweet rate than those that do not. **
- Tweets that contain less than 100 characters receive a 17% higher engagement than longer Tweets**
- The average Tweet has a life span of 2 hours***

Dan Zarrella, HubSpot
*** Buddy Media*
****Bill Faeth on Inbound Marketing Blog*

This research provides a good starting point for your strategy. As you get further involved, be sure to monitor your own businesses' engagement. You may find your followers' patterns to be different.

Now let's talk about content. Keeping up with website and social media postings can feel a bit overwhelming. Here are some tips to effectively manage your content.

> Not all content needs to be original. You can repost articles, Tweets, blogs and videos from other sources.

Set up a Google alert that will feed you a daily supply of news based on your key word selections. If you own a liquor store, for example, you can set up Google alerts for cocktails, cocktail trends, bars in your city, articles on wine, etc. This will provide you with daily feeds of articles and news on these topics which you are free to share on your social media platforms.

Your webmaster may be able to easily add your Facebook or Twitter feed to your homepage. This will automatically direct your posts to your website, adding new content regularly.

One of the easiest content additions is photography. Photos of new products, new daily specials, client news and store events all add depth to your brand and are quite easily incorporated into your website and social media on a regular basis.

Ask questions. Be silly. Pretend you have a friend on the other side.

Brainstorm content ideas with your staff. Are there questions that seem to be popping up with regularity from customers? Answer them on social media. Are there items you sell that seem to be universally loved? Feature them on social media. Interview your customers and post snippets with a photo. Ideas for content exist every minute of every day.

Inspiration

Here's a list of general posting ideas I've either used with clients or garnered from other resources. Even if they may not appear to be specifically geared to your business category, think of ways they might be adapted to work perfectly for you. Open your mind and have fun!

Special deals for social media followers only
      Share and get a deal
      Check in and get a deal

Ask questions
      Which would you choose? (Item A or B?)
      What's your favorite comfort food?
      What's the next color scheme for your living room?

Fill in the blank
I feel _____ when I eat a chocolate truffle.

Behind the scenes
Posts of staff doing everything from opening the store, unpacking inventory, serving customers to leaving exhausted at the end of the day. Make it fun and give people insight into the lengths you go to make your store great.

Your manufacturing process – if you make something proprietary, post photos of the process, i.e. jewelry or chocolate making, food preparation.

Do a poll
Get your questions answered right from the source.

Create a regularly scheduled feature
"Something of the day or week" (a flavor, a product, a tip, a dinner special)
Motivational quote of the day

Drive impulse purchases
It's raining out today. Ten percent off to anyone who braves the weather to come visit us.
We've got _____ left and want to sell them today. Come in and receive 20% off.

Announcements
New arrivals
New window displays
Employee of the week or month
Any press, publicity or awards received

Acknowledgement
To an employee for doing a great job
Congratulate a customer for an achievement – tag customer

Seasonal/Holiday
In addition to the usual holidays, focus on some offbeat holidays like National Cat Day to create interest
Don't forget your own store anniversary and milestones

Sales and Events
Promote. Promote. Promote.

Employees
Introduce them with profiles and credentials
Have them post from their perspective

Advice/How-To Information
Write your own how-to tips and invite other experts to participate
as well

Charities
Post and promote your favorite charities
Host a virtual fundraiser
> Donate a dollar amount for every repost or share in a
> specified period of time.

Contests
Give followers the opportunity to win something by sharing,
answering a question or providing an email address.

Vote
We're thinking of adding this to our selection. Yes or no?

Sneak Peak/Teasers
Tease followers in advance of a new product introduction or special
announcement.

Cross promotions
Promote your strategic partners

In general, use a combination of entertainment, education and sales offers. Use photos, illustrations and videos to create interest. And yes, it's okay to post an occasional joke or cute pet photo.

Restaurants and food establishments have a unique posting opportunity by capitalizing on the trend of posting food photos. If I owned a restaurant I would mandate that when a server saw diners taking photos of their food, they approach the table and offer the guests a free dessert (or some other offering) to post the photo to social media, identifying the restaurant, on the spot. By not doing so, you're missing a huge content opportunity!

As I was writing this, I took a few minutes to look at my Facebook page. One of my clients opened a third location today and posted, "thanks to everyone for coming out" with a photo of a man. It went on to read, "And thanks to this man who was our first customer." Seriously? No name? No identification of their first customer? Had they identified and tagged him, all his friends would have seen the post and spread the word of their new store.

Here's the last word on posting. Don't be afraid to try something. The worst that happens is no one remembers it a few hours later. Or maybe, just maybe, it intrigues your followers and opens some new doors.

A few ideas and resources to make social media management easier
Even with the best of intentions, the daily management of social media can often take a back seat to other duties. The best strategy is to plan out your postings a week to a month in advance. If you set aside some time to think about what you're going to say and do it ahead of time, it will eliminate that daily pressure. By creating a posting schedule, you can delegate the actual posting duty to your staff. (Remember, someone does have to monitor your accounts and respond as well.)

There are some terrific tools available that allow you to write and schedule posts in advance. Just set them up and they'll automatically post on the date selected. Two great options for this service are:

HootSuite (www.hootsuite.com)
Provides an entire social media management platform.

Snap Retail (www.snapretail.com)
Offers posting ideas for emails and social media centered around themes and includes related artwork.

Both are reasonably priced tools that can expedite and enhance your social media strategy.

If you are serious about using a contest to increase your fan base, take a look at Heyo, www.heyo.com and Woohoo, www.woohoo.com. They both provide automated tools to help you easily create contests, sweepstakes and other social media promotions along with analytics, training and advice.

ACTION ITEM #8
Social Media

Select the social media platforms you believe will work best for your business and target market.
Facebook
Twitter
Instagram
Pinterest
YouTube/Video
LinkedIn
Blogging

More internet-based options

Pay per click advertising

Pay per click (PPC) ads are paid online ads. When someone does a search using selected keywords, ads reflecting those keywords will show up with "sponsored" or "ad" above them. They generally appear above or to the right of the organic search results, depending on the search engine.

PPC ads are attractive because:
- You only pay if someone clicks on your ad.
- You can set a monthly budget, say $100, and once you're ad has been clicked enough times to fulfill that budget, the campaign automatically ends.
- Results are measurable in real time.

- You can select the demographic target, time of day and geographic location in which you want your ads to be served.

To purchase PPC ads, select relevant keywords people might use when searching for a business like yours. For example, a fabric store might select keywords like sewing, fabric and crafts. Some keywords cost pennies per click, others much more depending on their popularity. With some providers you may have to enter into a competitive bidding situation to determine the price for each click, or, on sites like Amazon, you pay a flat rate based on the keyword(s) you select. You are charged that amount each time someone clicks on your ad. Let's say your keywords cost $1 each. You can set a monthly budget of $50, and once your ad is clicked 50 times, whether it takes one day or thirty, your buy is complete.

The purpose of PPC ads is to drive traffic to your website or get the phone to ring. So if you decide to use this platform, be sure the link from your ads directs visitors to a landing page that clearly addresses their needs. Also be warned, the selection of keywords will take some tweaking so don't expect to get it right the first time. Unless you have a solid lead capture device or are selling items online, you may not get the maximum benefit out of an expenditure on PPC ads.

Reputation management

Reputation management is a relatively new opportunity – and concern -for retailers. One of the biggest complaints I get from owners is, *"Negative Yelp reviews are killing me!"* Whether you're being reviewed on Yelp, Urbanspoon, Google, Yahoo, Trip Advisor or any local sites, reviews can create buzz or turn prospects away. Either way, review sites play an extremely important role in today's retail business. Consider this. According to ZMOT:

- 73% of people trust online reviews as much as a recommendation from a friend or family members.
- Businesses with 6 or more positive reviews enjoy higher Google, Yahoo and Bing search rankings than their competitors.
- 87% of potential customers click on businesses with 3 star or higher ratings.

You can manage your online reputation and use it to your advantage. I should say, you *must* control this aspect of marketing because of its growing importance. The good news is, if your business is doing the right thing, there won't be much to manage except to encourage your happy customers to write reviews and thank them for doing so.

The biggest issues I see with clients regarding reputation management:

1. Ignoring the process
2. Not asking for reviews
3. Belief that you need to pay Yelp to get positive reviews posted

Let's talk a little bit about Yelp first since it really is in the midst of a PR crisis with retailers and restaurants. Businesses are claiming they're being extorted - forced to pay for advertising- in order for Yelp to stop filtering positive reviews. None of this has been proven and much of it may be a misunderstanding. According to Yelp, their review posting policies have nothing to do with paid advertising and everything to do with the algorithms in place to filter out reviews deemed to be fake.

According to Localvox.com, Yelp looks at a variety of criteria and filters reviews that are:

> From someone who has only written one review (not an established Yelper)
>
> From someone who has no profile information
>
> Are short and lacking details

According to Yelp's website, "We're purposely not elaborating about all the variables that go into defining an "established" user, because it's a catch-22: the more descriptive we are about what makes an established user, the less effective our filter is at fighting shills and malicious content."

Unfortunately, this filtering process isn't perfect and sometimes, legitimate reviews - good and bad- are filtered, too. From your perspective, responding to reviews, adding the reviewer as a Yelp friend, connecting and voting the review as "Useful" or "Funny" can help in posting status.

The one thing you never want to do is pay for a positive Yelp review. If Yelp determines this is the case you will be publicly flagged as a Yelp Review Cheater.

Managing your online reputation

Let's go back and do an online search for your business name once again. The results will show the online sites on which you are included or reviewed. First, "claim" each listing, and check that your address, phone and other details are correct. Post store hours. Put in a link to your website. Add photos. You even have the option on most to post an online coupon. Restaurants can link menus to their listings. Now you have improved your online visibility, so when people search for "women's apparel, Ft. Worth," for example, they will find the correct information about your store. They may also find an assortment of negative and positive reviews.

How will you now handle the upkeep of these sites? Who will monitor and respond to them? How often? Daily? Weekly?

> First, be sure to say thank you to those who sing your praises.

> Create a policy for handling negative reviews. Will you address them with an explanation or an apology via a post? Will you offer a refund or some sort of makeup experience?

> It's important to publicly address the issue. If you have a spate of negative reviews you need to look closely at your business and find out more about the problem. For example, you may find, upon closer examination, most of the negative comments are coming from people who bought a particular product or were served by a particular staff member. Don't just chalk up a negative review to an isolated incident or a disgruntled customer.

Given the importance of reviews in your overall online presence, you may want to consider some help in the form of a review platform like Reputationbiz.com. Reputationbiz automatically solicits reviews from customers and filters bad reviews before posting to major sites.

It gives you the opportunity to address the problem before it goes public and provides a host of other benefits including a microsite with all your reviews, further boosting your SEO.

Ecommerce and selling online

The business news is filled with stories about large retailers and their omni-channel marketing efforts. They are striving to strike the balance between face-to-face interaction and online sales. Many of you wonder if you should have an ecommerce component to your business. Understand that online selling brings with it a whole different set of challenges, including fulfillment, shipping and, of course, returns. It's really a business unto itself. Here are two barometers for helping you decide whether or not to sell online:

You have a proprietary product that can't be found elsewhere
> For example, my artisan chocolate client, mentioned earlier, developed a Chocolate of the Month club online.

Your core business is stabilized
> Best to focus on solidifying your bricks and mortar business before taking on the distraction of a new venture.

There are a couple of ways you might want to test the waters for online selling that are low risk and low cost.

Facebook store – There are now a number of apps that allow you to set up a virtual storefront on Facebook. Shopify (www.shopify.com)

and Ecwid (www.ecwid.com) provide store platforms at monthly costs starting at no charge for a basic storefront.

EBay

You can always try selling on EBay to test demand for your product. If you begin getting traction in either of these areas, you may want to consider a larger ecommerce effort.

ACTION ITEM # 9
Additional online tools
Evaluate these internet based opportunities on the worksheet.

PPC Advertising
I think this option is right for my business and would like to investigate it further
I am currently using PPC advertising and would like to continue testing
I don't think PPC ad is a good choice for my business at this time

Reputation Management
My online reviews are generally positive and I monitor and respond to the review sites regularly
The quantity and star rating of my online reviews could be improved
My online reviews are generally negative
I have not paid attention to the online review sites

Ecommerce/Online sales
Online sales may be an option for me to consider for growing sales
Online sales are not a priority at this time

CHAPTER 15

Traditional Advertising

With the exception of email marketing, this chapter will review offline advertising and promotional opportunities, what might be referred to as traditional advertising. Once again, we'll review the various channels, what they're designed to do and how they work together to help you grow small.

Email marketing

Despite its insane growth and the general annoyance that a full inbox can bring, email marketing is still a formidable marketing tool, especially given the fact it's virtually free. Why then, are so many retailers not taking full advantage of this amazing opportunity to connect with customers and prospects? Yes, like everything in your marketing toolbox, it takes planning and strategy development but the rewards can be great. You need to put email marketing at the top of your to do list.

Creating your database

To start, you need to have a database of email addresses. If you don't collect customer email addresses in store, start today. Many of you indicate you get some resistance in this step. It's true, not everyone wants to receive your emails, but don't let the minority discourage you from reaching out to those who will welcome your communication.

There are two easy strategies to collect emails from customers:

1. Ask for an email at first purchase
   Use a hook. *"I see you're a first time customer. We really appreciate your business and would like to email you a special offer to return."* Be sure to set up an autoresponder in your email system that kicks out a special offer to this new customer or send it manually.

2. Collect emails as part of the checkout process.
   Offer to email a receipt (many of the chains are doing this now) or have a screen set up on your credit card terminal so customers can input their email address before finishing the transaction.

Getting emails from visitors who don't buy is a little trickier but train your salespeople to make it part of their customer communication. You might use a similar approach as with first time customers, *"I'm sorry you didn't find anything that suited you today but we'd love to have you come back. Please share your email and we'll send you a discount coupon you can use during your next visit."*

The real key to successfully growing a database is staff training and making it part of the everyday interaction with customers.

Housing your database

You'll need to use an emailing system to send email blasts without being shut down by your Internet provider. Your POS or web platform may have this capability or you can use services like Constant Contact or MailChimp, which charge a modest monthly fee and provide free email templates and analytics as well.

Segmenting your database

There's another amazing and free opportunity to make your emails even more effective and that's by segmenting your database. You can keep separate databases and send unique messages to each. A home décor store might have separate databases for interior designers vs. retail customers. You might segment by gender (remember our example of the men's hair salon that sold the majority of its gift certificates to women?), category of items purchased and lead sources.

Think about your customer profile and what you'd like to accomplish through email marketing. Let's say you find you have a significant group of customers who buy only sale items. You might consider sending them an advance notice of a sale event to offer them the best selection and possibly encourage a higher average sale. Alternatively, you could send them first notices of new arrivals to entice them to begin buying at full price.

Segment your database to compliment your overall marketing strategy. Chances are, by sending a more targeted message, you'll increase your open rates and ultimately, store traffic as a result.

Using email marketing to Grow Small

Set a regular schedule for your emails – weekly or biweekly, but not less than monthly.

Create a standard template so recipients will begin to recognize your emails. The template should include your logo, store address, phone and hours, a "forward" button, and links to your website and social media sites.

Email content

Email marketing is not just about sending information on sales and special offers. Quite the opposite. It's about building a relationship with your customers and prospects. What can you include in your emails that a person would miss if they stopped receiving it? Will you feature product shots? An informative article? A video? How often will the emails contain an offer? Will the offer be exclusive to those on the email list? Will you have an employee, item or tip of the month or any other recurring feature? Keep the format of the content relatively standard in each email and make it relevant and interesting.

Subject lines

A great subject line will help increase your open rate. Keep them short and provocative. "News from the Beauty Shoppe" won't grab anyone's attention. "How to look 10 years younger in 30 minutes" might. Don't use all caps. EVER!

Personalize

Email services allow you to personalize each email with the recipient's name providing they are input into the database correctly. Take advantage of this feature. A personal email is more compelling than one that feels like it's been blasted to thousands.

Have you ever ordered from Zappos? Their email correspondence gives you a reason to smile. When you register, their subject line of their welcome email says, "Welcome and thanks for registering…We heart you! Inside, they write, "Let the good times begin" and list the benefits of ordering from Zappos. When you return an item (remember, return shipping is free) here are some snippets from your return confirmation: "We wanted to let you know that your return is back safe and sound in our warehouse. That trip over the river and through the woods to grandmother's house went smoothly. We are currently getting that eagerly awaited refund spruced up to head on back to you."

It's light. It's fun. And it definitely conveys their brand personality. You can create that same type of customer relationship with your email marketing – all at no cost.

Video email marketing

Video email is a relatively new marketing tool and an opportunity to really set yourself apart from the crowd. It's simply a matter of embedding short videos into your emails so when the recipient opens it, your video message greets them. Using video allows recipients to see, feel and hear the passion you have for your product or service.

An abundance of research overwhelmingly suggests that videos on a website or in emails will increase sales anywhere between 30 -100 percent.

Video email vs. static email
- Recipients spend 44% more time on video email
- Recipients share and forward video emails 41% more often
- Video emails have a 55% increase in click through rates
- Companies using video in email experience, on average, 40% higher revenue in a month than those companies that do not employ video

You don't need to be a pro to generate buzz using videos in email. You can create and edit a short (sixty seconds or less) video using your smartphone or tablet.

Right about now, I'm sure you have 2 questions.
How do I do this?
What kind of videos should I shoot?

I'm going to refer you to a short and easy tutorial on creating video for email marketing at www.tenantmentorship/com/growingsmallvideoemail. It includes detailed instructions and a host of inspirational ideas on the types of videos to create.

Here's a short list of video ideas to get your creative juices flowing. Think about how you can adapt these concepts for your business.

Style an outfit
Chef preparing an appetizing preparation of tonight's special
Makeovers/Before and After's
Exercise/Flavor/Special of the day/week/month
Health and wellness tips
How-to demonstrations

Introduction of a new product or service

Sales and event announcements

Birthday greeting to customers

Contests

A tour of your store

These are just a few of the ways you can use video. With a little imagination, you and your smart phone can set your business world on fire – and have fun doing it!

Whether you choose to use video or not, open a consistent line of compelling communication with your prospects via email.

Daily deal advertising

Daily deal advertising has made its way into mainstream marketing. Every day, businesses large and small are enticing potential customers to buy well-priced deals via Groupon, Living Social, Gilt and an array of similar local sites. Daily deal platforms can create mass exposure for your business and, if you're not careful, send you into a spiral of discounting. They seem to be the default attraction when businesses are new or struggling and a poorly executed daily deal can actually hurt rather than help.

I find many small retailers and restaurants enamored with the platform. And why not? There's no upfront cost, which is very appealing, your message is delivered to thousands of subscribers and it's easy to implement. For those of you who don't know the inner workings of daily deals, it's quite simple. You offer 50 percent or more off your pricing and split the remaining 50 percent with the daily deal platform. That leaves you earning 25 percent of the total retail price.

The very first thing you need to consider is whether or not that 25 percent, *at minimum,* covers your hard costs. I have seen businesses receive 200, 400, 600 or more Groupons for dinner or merchandise and lose money on each and every one of them! That's not a good plan, especially considering there's the possibility the people using these discounts are already your customers or may not convert to regular customers. We all love a good deal and daily deal audiences often just follow the discount, not the store. The nail salon industry is plagued by this problem. There is an entire contingency of women out there who only get their mani/pedi's using the abundantly available daily deal discounts!

Daily deal tips for Growing Small

Carefully consider the behavior you want to reward when creating your deal. The objective is not to give away stuff for free. You want to insure that anyone using that daily deal either:

1. Spends more money once in your store
2. Converts to a regular customer

The offer

Be strategic. Are you going to offer a dollar value ($20 for $40 worth of merchandise?) or a specific offer (a $40 product for $20)? If you offer a specific product, there may not be an opportunity to upsell because the customer may just come in and purchase the specified product and no more. If you offer $40 worth of merchandise for $20, however, and your average item is about $45, there's an opportunity to make more money.

Don't be afraid to think big when it comes to your deals

Try bundling items or services into a larger, more expensive package.

The makeup store I mentioned earlier was introducing eyelash extensions to their service menu. They didn't have a client base for this so a daily deal offer made sense for the exposure. Instead of just offering a one-time eyelash extension application, they packaged the service into a 6-month program: the original eyelash extension application plus touchups every three weeks. By increasing the size of the package they were not only getting more money, they were insuring these customers would be revisiting their store multiple times which, statistically, should improve the odds of them making additional purchases.

Collect emails for every deal redeemed

Your last step is to be able to communicate with these new customers after the sale to attempt to convert them into loyal fans. Get their emails when redeeming certificates. This is a must! That way, you'll be able to put them in your email database, communicate with them regularly and hopefully, earn their future business.

Advertising

Newspaper. Magazine. TV. Radio. Are any of them for you? These more traditional channels can enhance your business if used *correctly*.

Here's a typical conversation I have with clients about advertising.

Me: Do you advertise?
Client: Yes.
Me: Tell me about your advertising plan.
Client: Well, I put an ad in the local paper and it didn't work.
Me: When did you do that?
Client: When I first opened.
Me: Did you have an offer in the ad?

Client: No.
Me. Did you run it multiple times?
Client: No.
Me: How do you know it didn't work?
Dead silence.

Typically, I find the small business owner will select a media (local newspaper or magazine, perhaps cable TV), place an ad once or twice or run the cable spots for a week or two, have the media provider create the ad or spot and then wait for customers to break down the doors. The end result is inevitably, disappointment.

Media advertising can help in one of two ways:
      As a long term branding plan
      A short term promotional play

Unless you have the budget for a long term brand campaign, I strongly suggest you limit your use of traditional media to sales and promotions and use coupons or other tracking mechanisms to judge performance.

Without an offer or coupon, you'll be running branding ads. A brand awareness campaign is wonderful except you need to adjust expectations. No one will walk in the door holding your ad. You'll have to track calls, traffic and revenue to determine if you see a bump over the period of time the ads run, but you won't necessarily be able to track revenue back to the ads. If you do have a substantial budget, I highly recommend you hire a professional to assist in determining how to best spend that budget and to execute innovative creative to maximize its impact.

Advertising tips for Growing Small

Get educated

I'm sure media reps come to your door almost daily singing the praises of their particular vehicle. Take it all in. Read their media kits. Do an analysis against your targeted demo. See what your competition is doing and compare. Get the facts and decide which media will work best for you.

Make media reps your best friends

A seasoned media rep is often extremely knowledgeable about their publication or station and can provide you with insider information. Ask them for success stories or see if they can identify the types of ads or spots that are producing results for their clients.

Create a budget before you buy

Decide on your annual or quarterly media budget. Will you be advertising 12 months a year? Just during the holidays? For specific sales and events? Once you have a budget, you can determine the size and frequency of ads that will fit into your budget.

Size and frequency do matter

If you are considering running a one-time ad, please do me a favor and send the money to charity. It will serve a better purpose. If you are going to use advertising for visibility and branding purposes, purchase the largest ad you can afford to run a minimum of 8 to 12 weeks. It takes that long for your message to register with potential customers.

As far as ads go, I hate to be the bearer of bad news but size does matter. Those teeny tiny ads are generally relegated to the back of the publication, surrounded by bad ads and really aren't going to help your business. I find clients seem to gravitate to this least expensive option and quite frankly, you're probably not getting value for your money. Small ads can work but they need to be great either creatively/ visually or with an amazing, not-to-be-ignored offer!

Partner up

Try co-oping ads with a neighbor or two in your shopping center to share costs. You can do this as a branded play or as a joint promotion.

I worked with a high end shoe store and a neighboring cosmetics store. They ran joint ads in the local upscale city magazine. Their message was, "Making you look good from head to toe." Because they shared the cost they were able to run a respectably sized ad with greater frequency.

Special offers and sales

If you're going to run a short term schedule for a sale or event that contains a special offer, be sure to code the lead source into your POS so you can track results.

Focus on solid design/concept and a singular message

You may be using the graphic designer at your local publication or the production team at the cable or radio station to produce your ads. They typically produce your creative at little or no charge. Sometimes they have talented people working in production. Sometimes they don't. Take a look at the vehicle you choose and you'll get a good idea of the quality of the advertising they're producing. Let them show you samples of their work.

An ad or spot needs to focus on a singular message for the greatest impact. By showing multiple products or offers or discounts, you make the ad confusing and ineffective. Think about how you want to visually convey your brand and the singular message you want people to receive. Please don't create your own print ad on your computer.

Direct mail/direct response

Often effective, sometimes expensive, direct mail is an opportunity to bring your message directly into the mailboxes of a specific geographic or demographic target. If you know your current customer makeup, direct mail can help connect you to potential new customers with a similar profile. If you have a more general business, you can simply blanket a selected geographic area with your message.

If you want to design, produce and mail your own stand-alone piece, you'll need a database. Will you be mailing to your own database or purchase one based on your specifications? Direct mail houses sell mailing lists that can be refined by gender, income, zip code, household income and other filters. The more filters you choose, the more expensive the database. Sometimes, your purchase of these lists is for a one time use only so be sure to fully understand what you're buying before you sign up. (Check out www.infousa.com and www.experian.com to start your database research.)

In addition to the database purchase, costs to complete the mailing will include printing, mail house services and postage. Given the expense, be sure you have a solid offer and a great mailer to send. Online printers like www.psprint.com offer a full turnkey service to print and mail your piece using your own or a purchased list.

In its purest form, direct response advertising is a printed piece that is mailed to a database of targeted prospects. Today, there are a few additional options available.

Bundled coupon mailers

Services like Valpak or Money Mailer bundle your coupons with dozens of others and mail them to all households within desired zip codes. Typically, you'll find service businesses like rug cleaning and pest control companies utilizing this platform, but you may also find doctors, optical stores and restaurants as well. These mailers are generally discount driven and unless you're prepared to get into a price war, this channel probably isn't for you.

United States Post Office

The USPS has a program called Every Door Direct Mail (EDDM). You provide the post office a printed piece to their specifications and based on your purchase of specific zip code routes, they deliver it by carrier directly into the recipient's mail box. Because they are not postmarked, you avoid the expense of a mail house or other third party services, making it very affordable. There are printers who are EDDM partners that will take care of the entire process for you if you choose.

Here are few more direct mail tactics.

The old fashioned letter

Snail mail has truly fallen out of style and just the sheer delight of receiving a letter or a note card from a local business might just get someone's attention.

Friend-to-friend letter

I stole this from my political friends who send letters to their supporters asking them, in turn, to mail letters to their friends in support of the candidate. You can put your own twist on this by providing referral cards and ask your good customers to distribute them to their friends and family as a way to introduce new customers to your store.

"We miss you" letter

Track customers who haven't visited for a certain period and send them a "We miss you" letter or postcard along with an incentive to return. You can easily do this via email, but as mentioned earlier, the novelty of receiving a piece of mail can make it more impactful.

Field Marketing

Field marketing is a nice way to say door-to-door distribution. Depending on your neighborhood and type of business, field marketing might make sense. Hire high school or college students to distribute flyers door- to- door. Again, be strategic.

I have had pizza delivery stores do very well by distributing flyers on a Friday afternoon, in time for the weekend. An ice cream store distributed flyers to businesses in the area promoting lunchtime offers to fill in their slow time before kids got out of school.

Advertising of any sort costs money. The good news is, unlike years ago, it's not the only option for promoting business. When you are in a position to fully fund a smart advertising campaign, carefully create, plan and measure to achieve long term results.

ACTION ITEM #10
Traditional advertising
Please answer these questions on the worksheet.

Which advertising channels, if any, are appropriate for your business?

> Email marketing (This must be incorporated
> into your plan)
> Video email marketing
> Daily deal advertising
> Newspaper
> Magazine
> TV/Cable
> Radio
> Direct Mail
> Field marketing

I have a quarterly or annual advertising budget allocated

I currently using some of these channels and need to better monitor their effectiveness.

CHAPTER 16

Promotions And Events

Put on your creative caps because this is where it gets fun. In the world of grassroots marketing, promotions and events reign supreme. They involve working on a hyper-local, hyper-segmented level and when innovative and well-planned, promotions not only help attract new customers, they can also create buzz and publicity in your community.

There are a number of types of promotional events to consider.

In-store and proprietary promotions
- Events you plan independently or with a partner and host in your facility
- Contests, giveaways, sweepstakes or other programs, generally held over a period of time, that may involve registration, nomination or other participation and culminate in an event or the selection of winners

Third party/off-site/sponsorships

- Landlord-sponsored events in your center
- Community, sporting, business or special interest events at which you exhibit or sponsor
- Expos, fairs, green markets

Charitable promotions

- Partnering with a charity to drive business

Price driven promotions

- Offering discounts to drive traffic and sales

Let's review each different type of promotion to see what's right for your business.

In-store events and proprietary promotions

Who doesn't love the idea of bringing new people right to your door? An on-site event is one of the best grassroots tactics in the retailer's toolbox. It's a fantastic way to introduce new folks to your brand, show them a positive and unique experience and hopefully, convert them into loyal customers. Remember, an in-store event isn't always about bringing in huge numbers of people to your store or restaurant, it's about bringing in the *right* people!

Creating an event requires detailed planning and advance promotion. The last thing you want is for something to go wrong or worse yet-have no one show up.

Here are a few of the typical events you see at many local retailers:
>   Private VIP events
>   Classes/seminars
>   Makeovers
>   Wine tastings
>   Girl's Night Out
>   Trunk shows

While these are fine, I'd like to encourage you to try to kick things up a notch by creating a promotion that's a bit more unusual and interesting. Remember, the event doesn't necessarily have to be related to your business, just relevant to your audience. By knowing your customer's interests (refer to your customer profile) you could:

> Create an event series that brings people with similar interests together like monthly book club meetings.

> Put a new twist on an old idea. For example, organize an Easter egg hunt for adults with fabulous hidden prizes. A jewelry store could put a diamond in one of the eggs.

> Create an unusual celebration. Mozart loved coffee. A coffee shop could hold a Classical Music and Coffee Tasting event.

> Turn a need into a promotion. Do you need some great photography and can't afford a professional photographer? Why not hold a photography contest in which local professionals or amateurs can take photos

of your product and win exposure in your store, on your website and through your social media for a year?

Proprietary promotions are also designed to create buzz but aren't limited to one time or in-store events.

Examples of proprietary promotions:

Upscale men's-only salon

Held a "Win a Makeover for your Dad" promotion for Father's Day. People were asked to submit a short essay about their dad or husband. Nominees were featured on the salon's Facebook page during the course of the contest which received some local press.

Multiple winners received a makeover. The Grand Prize winner received a prize package worth $1,000 including gifts from partners (a golf course, a men's clothing store, a restaurant). Before and after photos of the winner were posted on the salon's Facebook page and website.

Cosmetics store

Women were invited to come in for free makeovers during the contest period. Before and after photos were taken of each participant and emailed to them for posting on their personal Facebook pages. The person who received the most Facebook likes would win a fabulous vacation so the photos essentially went viral in an attempt to garner votes. The store also posted the photos regularly to Facebook. The winner

was announced at a glamorous on-site event attended
by the participants, their friends and customers.

Proprietary promotions have multiple layers and multiple opportunities
for publicity and community impact.

Third party/off-site/sponsorships

By participating in or sponsoring someone else's event, you can gain
exposure without having to do all the organizing and planning.
Example of third party events:

- Marathons, races and sporting events
- Chamber or community organization expos and fundraising
  galas
- Landlord-sponsored events in your center

Let's start with the last one first. Not too many landlords are
organizing marketing events these days but if you happen to be
fortunate enough to be in one of these centers, make the most of this
terrific opportunity. Oddly enough, most of the clients I work with
who are in such centers actually complain about the promotions.

> *They hold them on the other side of center so it doesn't
> benefit me.*
> *The people who come aren't my target.*
> *I don't get any business from them.*

Quite frankly, if you're not getting results from these gatherings, you
really need to look at the quality of your participation. Whether the
event brings 100 or 10,000 people to your center, it's hard to believe
you can't find a way to attract new customers.

Are you truly participating or simply putting brochures or products on a table and expecting magic?

Are you sampling, handing out bouncebacks, collecting emails, holding a drawing? How are you making yourself and your brand memorable?

Are you waiting for people to walk in your door or are you finding a way to court them for future business?

Truth be told, the visitors to these events are not necessarily there to see you. Your job, then, is to find a way to get them interested enough to come back.

I have a number of clients in a particular center that holds a movie night weekly during the summer. Each Friday evening, hundreds of young families gather on the green to watch an outdoor movie. At the time I began working with several stores in this center, not one of them took the time to go out into that audience. What a missed opportunity! We developed bounceback and sampling programs for each client that allowed them to make a meaningful impression on these visitors and boost future business.

In another center, the owner spends hundreds of thousands of dollars annually on hosting massive events monthly that draw anywhere from 1000 to 5000 visitors at a time. A bowling alley client complained the events brought them no business. Corny as it sounds, we purchased bowling ball and bowling pin costumes and had these characters mill through the crowd and hand out plastic cards with mystery amounts of value for use in the bowling alley's arcade. The fun of the costumes and the delight in the offer made the business memorable at the event without waiting for people to physically walk in the door.

And finally, I asked a beauty salon who never participated in center events to simply go outside into the crowd during a recent promotion and hand out 200 promotional flyers. They got 8 new clients the very next day!

If you have a landlord that is paying to bring visitors to your center, it's a gift. Most of the time participation is at no cost to you. Smart retailers need to take full advantage of the opportunity.

Additional tips for participating in third party events:

Negotiate the best benefits package possible. Whether exhibiting or sponsoring, try to get maximum exposure through signage, program ads and custom benefits.

Try to secure the database of attendees, if possible, for future marketing. If the organization won't release their database, you might be able to negotiate having them do an email blast for you.

Put coded bouncebacks in the goody bags.

Create unforgettable T-shirts for your staff so they're noticed at the event. Make up a song and dance. Do whatever it takes to rise above the noise of the rest of the participants.

Immediately follow up with each new contact then continue to connect with them as part of your regular marketing program.

Charitable/cause related promotions

You've probably been approached hundreds of times to participate with local charities and asked to do everything from donate merchandise for silent auctions to springing for sponsorship dollars, organizing walking teams and buying tables at banquets. Before you spend another dollar, take a minute to think about how you give your money, merchandise and time.

There are two ways to approach charitable giving. The first is altruistic. If you have a cause or passion in which you want to participate because it's meaningful to you, by all means, do so. This is not a business decision, it's one that comes from the heart. The second is using charitable involvement as a business builder. For the purposes of this discussion, we'll talk about the latter.

Let's start with merchandise donations. I highly recommend creating a budget and formal process for giving donations. This allows you to handle your giving gracefully and without creating bad feelings. You certainly don't want to offend representatives of local organizations by having them think you don't take your community participation seriously. After all, they may be potential customers. To avoid an uncomfortable situation, create a charitable donation request form for the organization to complete with their charity name, contact person, reason for the donation (i.e. silent auction, raffle, etc.), purpose of the charity, how long in business and their 501(c)3 number which a legitimate charity must have and finally, recognition you will receive for your donation. Explain to them:

> As a small business, you have an annual budget for
> charitable giving.
> All requests must be submitted using the form.
> You evaluate all requests monthly, make your choices
> and will notify them of your decision at that time.

Be sure to review these forms on a predetermined timetable and notify all applicants of your decision. The formal process will help mitigate bad feelings from the rejected parties and help you make the most of your charitable contributions.

Charitable partnerships
Local charities and not-for-profits represent a wonderful opportunity to do well by doing good. The first step is to find a local organization whose donor base represents or resonates with your core audience. For example, you may have a clientele of young mothers whose children all go to the same school. That school might be an excellent beneficiary of your charitable efforts.

Work on a mutually beneficial partnership with that organization that will provide them revenue in exchange for promotion on their part. In the example of the school, perhaps there are 500 children attending. You can offer those 500 sets of parents:

> A discount on merchandise during a specific time
> frame using a promo code and donate a percentage of
> all those purchases back to the group.

A percentage of sales generated from a signature product created just for the organization, i.e. a signature drink, cupcake, pancake, t-shirt or piece of jewelry.

Or you can have the charity create the signature product. For example, a pizza restaurant might invite local charities to create a specialty pizza to be judged by a non-biased panel. The winner's pizza will be made and sold for 30 days and proceeds from sales of that pizza will be donated back to the organization.

The opportunity to fundraise. If you sell items like candy, baked goods, gift items or handcrafted products, you can offer your local schools or boy and girl scout troops the opportunity to sell your product. They pre-sell the items at retail. Purchasers can pick up the merchandise at your store and you pay the organization a percentage of sales, preferably on a sliding scale to incentivize performance. For example:

  30% on sales up to $1,500

  40% on sales from $1,501-$5,000

  50% on sales of $5,001+

One of the easiest charitable fundraisers to implement is to simply sell an organization discounted gift certificates to your store. You sell them a $25 gift certificate for $15. They, in turn, resell it for $25. They raise money. You get business.

Sometimes a fundraiser can be driven by you, benefit a cause, but have no real affiliation with the charity itself. For example:

Heart Health Month – Make a donation for everyone who wears red or offer a percentage of sales for every red mani-pedi.

Dry cleaner or clothing store – Give customers a discount for donating used clothing at your store during a specified period and contribute the clothing to a local shelter.

Local charities bring with them great need and great supporters. By working together with them in a smart and strategic way, you can build goodwill for your store while building sales.

Small Business Events
Many communities host "shop local" promotions and these are important opportunities to embrace your status as an independent retailer. There are also two large national events in which you should participate.

American Express heavily promotes Small Business Saturday which takes place on the Saturday after Thanksgiving. The company incentivizes its cardholders to shop small on this day and provides retailers with posters, promotional ideas and even the opportunity to list their business on the Small Business Saturday website. www.americanexpress.com/shopsmall

The month of July is designated as Independent Business Month and the organizers of this event offer similar benefits and programs for small retailers to maximize their involvement. www.indieretailermonth.com

Given the importance of small business patronage, these are ready-made opportunities to herald your status in the community.

Price driven promotions

To discount or not, that's the question. Discounting used to be a lot simpler pre-recession. Items were sold at full price until they went on sale at regular intervals throughout the year. The post-recession economy and the proliferation of outlet and discount stores has altered this model and deep discounts have become the shopping norm.

Mom's and Pop's got on the discount bandwagon over these past years in an effort to keep their heads above water and now, well, it seems sales are simply an everyday occurrence. I work with too many stores that have sales every single weekend. It's hard to make your margins or get customers to buy full price when they're used to regular discounts.

Creating a discounting strategy

What's the real purpose of a sale or discount? There are three main motivations to reduce prices:
- To sell slow moving merchandise
- To bring in more customers/sell higher volumes
- To test the market or trial new merchandise or products

If you are discounting every week just to make (or try to make) your revenue numbers, it's time to reexamine your business model starting with your markups and margins. As one person so wisely described it to me, you can have a Tiffany or Walmart model. The first is to sell fewer items at a higher margin. The second is to sell a higher volume at a lower margin. Neither is right or wrong but you do need to decide where on the spectrum your business model falls and stick to it. Do you have the type of product and store concept that supports high-end pricing? Do you have the ability to buy at a price that will allow you to reduce prices and the volume of business to support a discount model?

Are you consistently putting items on sale because they're not selling or because you're overstocking? If you're buying too much merchandise and putting it on sale just to clear the shelves, you're not just hurting your margins, you're hurting cash flow. If items simply aren't selling, take a look at your sales by category to determine your best selling items and look for patterns to help you stock more of what your customer wants.

Quite frankly, when small stores start competing on a pricing play, they almost always lose. The role of a healthy independent retailer is to provide merchandise not necessarily available elsewhere and a level of service you won't find in a larger establishment. It's hard to do that and be a discount store too!

Here are a number of discount and sales strategies to consider:
> Annual clearance – a great opportunity to draw traffic with deep discounts one time each year. Promote it heavily and create customer anticipation.

> In and out days – I really like the idea of putting out new merchandise on a specific day of the week and moving a few items into a sale area on that same day. We've implemented this with a number of clients as New Merchandise Tuesday (their slowest day). They would only put new merchandise out on Tuesday and, as mentioned, move some items to the sale rack. It's a

great way to keep customers motivated to come back regularly and keep the store and sale area fresh.

When you do have a sale, put merchandise out at 20 or 30 percent off for a couple of days or a week – then slash. Get rid of it! There's nothing worse than a stale sale rack.

Create a sales calendar and stick to it rather than impulsively holding sales…

…except when there are situations in which you need to spontaneously discount. Remember earlier when we discussed KPI's indicating the month's revenues are behind? In situations like this you might consider an impromptu sale.

Are you trying to fill in a slow time? Maybe your Monday mornings are consistently slow. You can try to improve performance by holding specials or sales just on Monday mornings.

Is a particular item moving slowly or are you trying to test reaction to a new item or product line? Promote it as a weekly special.

Get away from entire store sales and try putting specific items or categories of items on sales instead.

Alternatives to sales

Think about the behavior you're trying to reward with sales. Perhaps you can encourage that behavior through alternate methods. For example:

Growing specific business segments

Rather than holding a sale, consider discounts that focus on underperforming segments of your business.

I worked with a fast food restaurant that was enjoying a robust lunch business, but after 2 pm, you could shoot a cannon in the place. We began handing out bouncebacks to lunch customers for a 20 percent discount off any purchase after 4 pm. Dinner business increased 25 percent in the first month.

Rewarding loyalty

In the service business, there's nothing better than knowing a client will come back regularly. You can begin offering a prebooking discount for making their next appointment on the spot.

Try combining a sale with a promotion. For example, host a Girls' Night Out event in which customers are rewarded with a discount for bringing a potential new customer to the event.

If you have a policy of regular discounting, you're probably cheating yourself out of a full price sale from a regular customer.

An Italian fast casual restaurant introduced gourmet pizza slices at a price of $4-$5 each. The owner decided to have a sale each Wednesday, selling slices for $1 to attract new customers. Sounds reasonable except *he did not promote this offer anywhere except for in-store signage which means the people who were taking advantage of the discount were those already coming to his store and ready to pay full price. His sales actually went down.*

Sales are an important aspect of retail but will only be a financial benefit if carefully planned and coordinated.

Using promotions to Grow Small

We've discussed a lot of promotional opportunities for your business, from small to blowouts! As you decide which ones might be right for you, remember an effective promotion starts with a great idea followed by flawless execution and ends with meticulous follow up. Promotional dollars and time invested need to have a measurable return on investment.

Inspiration

Here are more few more promotional ideas of all types to inspire you.

Create networking opportunities for your customers.

>	Host private "shop and network" in-store lunches
>	Cocktails and Connections- invite business people to network in your store

Join a Meet Up group or start one of your own focused around the interests of your typical customer.

Consider cross promotion opportunities with your neighbors. Buy here, get a discount there.

Offer an unforgettable, publicity worthy prize. For example, a jewelry store selling engagement rings might hold contest for men who are about to get engaged. The winner receives a billboard on which to post his proposal.

Pizza – deliver 5 free pizzas daily to local businesses to promote catering. The surprise of this free gift is sure to get attention!

Organize free stroller fitness or yoga classes to attract moms.

Create an "Of the Month" or subscription program to generate repeat business

---

ACTION ITEM #11
Promotions and Events
Please complete on the worksheet.

List promotions you are currently organizing along with budget and results.
>   Which promotions can be better executed?
>   Which should be eliminated?

What types of new promotions should you consider implementing?

Is it time to consider a new strategy for discounting and sales?

Would your business benefit from setting up a formal charitable donation request system?

Chapter 17

Public Relations

PR is the art of getting publicity for your business in magazines, newspapers and on TV news. In recent years, it has also grown to include exposure on relevant blogging sites. There are key differences in the types of exposure so let's examine them.

Press/News

Major daily newspapers and network TV news are editorial driven, meaning they only report on items that are current and newsworthy. Getting featured in a major daily or on TV news requires pitching a story that's timely, relevant and sometimes, exclusive to that particular media. You'll need to research the appropriate editor or reporter based on the angle of the story, i.e. small business, lifestyle or neighborhood focus, for example. Then frame your pitch to appeal to that particular type of editorial content.

Seeking publicity at this level is, quite frankly, best left to the professionals. Alternatively, I'm going to refer you to an excellent book, *Starring You! The Insiders' Guide to Using Television and Media to Launch Your Brand, Your Business and Your Life*, written by Marta Tracy and Terrance Noonan. It's a comprehensive guide to generating your own publicity and well worth the read.

One last thing to remember. True public relations as described above means you have no control over what's printed or reported. Sometimes, it can work against you.

Local TV

Local TV news and cable stations often have programs in which they feature local businesses. Check your local stations for shows and segments about small business, local entrepreneurs, new businesses and business people helping the community. They may also have segments related to your specific type of enterprise, for example, fashion, health and fitness, dining out or DIY projects. First, watch the show to get a sense of how they format their segments. Create a short and compelling pitch customized for that particular show and send it to the correct producer or reporter. Don't use a generic pitch or blanket multiple people at a station. That's a great way to insure your request will end up in the trash can.

Advertising driven media

Some publications are advertising driven, meaning they will provide a certain amount of "editorial" content about your business in exchange for a predetermined advertising expenditure. Even your local daily may occasionally have a special advertising section in which you receive an article along with your ad. You will be required to provide this editorial content so be sure it is well written and reads like a news article, not an ad.

Sometimes local publications, generally weeklies, invite business owners to write a regular or occasional column. Check to see if there's an opportunity to create this type of relationship in your area. Understand that you will have to provide an interesting column on deadline that can't and shouldn't be sales pitches, but rather, an opportunity to showcase your expertise. The byline will be your calling card. Of course, if you should secure this type of arrangement, you can use the column as content for your own website, email, blog and social media to further spread the word.

"Best of" issues

Your city magazine or alternative weekly newspaper probably has an annual "Best of" Issue, in which they identify, by nomination from the general public, the best businesses in various categories. The winners are selected by the voting public. Yes, it's a popularity contest. Nonetheless, these issues provide excellent exposure for the winners, along with the opportunity to brand your business as a "best of" in your city. Research your local media to find out which has a "best of" issue and participate. If you choose to do so, you'll have to make a commitment to engage customers, friends and family to maximize your votes over the contest period. You can do this in-store and of course, on your website and through social media.

Awards

Typically, chambers of commerce and other community organizations hold annual business of the year and woman/man of the year awards. The underlying goal of these events is to raise money and they count on the nominees to actively help promote them. Nominate yourself or ask someone else to nominate you. Then get on committee and embrace the process. Show up for the planning meetings and do some high level networking. Buy a table at the event and bring a team of vocal cheerleaders. Take an ad in the program and announce your nomination through all your communication channels.

Of course, if you should win, shout it from the rooftops. There is nothing greater than third party acknowledgement to build credibility and awareness for you and your business.

Bloggers

This is a relatively new outlet for promotion and the opportunities grow each day. Most blogs focus on certain topics (fashion, parenting, crafts, etc.) Some simply report information, others require payment to review your store or product. You can research local blogs via a Google search. Read the blogs to determine which are appropriate outlets for your business. Do they have engaged followers? Can you benefit from the exposure? Recently, a client of mine had their product reviewed on a blog (for a fee) which resulted in 500 new Facebook likes. Blogs can be powerful promoters of your business.

There are any number of opportunities for exposure in your community via publicity channels. How will you utilize them to grow small?

ACTION ITEM # 12

Public Relations

Please complete on the worksheet.

What local public relations channels are available to you?

Which do you think might benefit your business?

CHAPTER 18

The People Factor

What's the value of a customer? The actual sale you make today? Future sales? What is one good customer worth to you?

Getting customers is one thing. Keeping them coming back is another and here's the great news: maintaining customer loyalty doesn't require any money – just a plan.

Customer loyalty programs

A 2014 study reported that only 16 percent of businesses believe they have a highly effective loyalty program. Only 54 percent of respondents said they could calculate the revenue impact of those programs. You should note the surveys went out to companies of $50 million plus in annual revenue, but as a small business you have the flexibility to create a more vibrant and interesting kind of customer loyalty program – and measure its impact every single day!

To start, let's get away from the frequent purchaser punch card mentality. It's transactional at best. Think a little more innovatively about your customer (remember, we now have a customer profile) and what type of reward would be meaningful to them and fit in your budget.

One idea that seems to gain a lot of traction with customers is a program that offers a rotating series of benefits. For example, if a customer met the purchase or point goal at your store this month, they might receive a gift certificate to the restaurant next door. Next month, it might be a free shampoo and blow dry from the salon down the street. Another month, it might be a donation to their favorite charity. You might even choose to create a unique event or provide services as a benefit like inviting the top ten purchasing customers to an elegant dinner catered by a partnering restaurant and held right in your store. The changing list of benefits inspires customers to pay attention to the program because there's always a new reward!

Enlist your shopping center neighbors or other businesses to provide benefits for your loyalty programs. These partnerships will not just benefit your store, it will promote new visits to your partners' businesses as well. Whatever benefits you choose, just be sure they're relevant to the customer.

Points and gifts aren't the only ways to build customer loyalty. You can use your POS to track customer preferences and send out, "You might also like…." emails showing similar or related merchandise to the ones the customer already purchased. (Online stores do this extremely effectively and you can too!) You can also use customer preference information to notify them when something new comes in that tracks against their taste and buying habits.

Always be sure to set up an autoresponder email to thank customers each and every time they make a purchase. This type of post-sale communication can work wonders to keep your store top of mind. It's also a great time to ask them to follow you on social media and to write an online review.

Communicate with your VIP membership regularly through an email newsletter. Depending on your business, the newsletter can include tips, news about customers who have benefited from the loyalty program and even articles from outside experts related to your business category. Communication with your loyal customers is key to making them feel valued and create a very personal relationship – even when they're not in your store.

Let's give them something to talk about

Wouldn't it be great to have a team of people out on the street singing the praises of your business? Well you can. And it won't cost you a dime.

For a consumer, nothing is more powerful than a personal recommendation from someone they know, like and trust. So it's time to put your fans to work for you. Please don't confuse this with word-of-mouth which infers that you are not in control of the process - that you are waiting for others to talk about you. In our growing small plan, we can put together an ambassador program which you control to build all-important relationships and enjoy the power of multiplication!

Cultivating ambassadors

Identify customers, friends and family who are loyal and devoted fans and develop formalized referral programs that benefit all involved. Here's one very simple idea that has worked remarkably well for my clients.

Print a quantity of business cards to hand out to your fans that say something like this:

We love having you as a customer and quite frankly, we'd like more just like you. Please let your friends know about us by giving them this card. They'll receive a 20 percent discount on their first purchase and when we receive two back with your name on it, you'll automatically receive a 20 percent discount on your next purchase as well.

Give these cards to your staff to hand out to all your best customers and watch what happens*!*

Strategic alliances

Like ambassadors, alliances are an effective means of cross marketing with businesses and organizations that already reach people who match your customer profile. So, for example, a shoe store might partner with a clothing boutique, a home décor store with a paint store or architect. Once you've identified the correct partners (yes, you can and should have multiple alliances) create a structured program.

Meet with your partner to create a program that benefits both of you. This isn't a one way street. Nor is it simply a matter of putting your partner's business cards on your checkout. An alliance must be promoted and tracked for effectiveness.

Badly trained customers

We all have them. Time bandits who suck the minutes or even hours out of our day. People who never purchase anything unless it's at a deep discount. Those who continue to shop at your store yet complain every time they come in. You know who I'm talking about. I know it's frustrating, but quite frankly, you've allowed them to get away with this behavior. Now you have to retrain them.

Here are a few examples of badly trained customer situations I've worked with:

Breakfast restaurant – consistently promoted 99 cent breakfast coupons and over the years, nearly 80 percent of their very unprofitable breakfast business was dining for under a buck!

Italian restaurant - allowed customers to use discount coupons on top of the early bird pricing rendering the profit from that business at virtually zero.

Cartridge refill company – in a desperate effort to keep customers, would deliver $10 ink cartridges anytime, anywhere, regardless of the size of the order.

Mother of the Bride dress store – would spend an unlimited amount of time with customers who couldn't make up their minds and ultimately, didn't buy.

What can you do with these badly trained customers? Fire them! I know that sounds crazy. You're thinking, *"Wait a minute, I can't afford to lose business!* But think about it. You're really not losing anything. In the case of the restaurants, the business was simply unprofitable. In both the instances above, we pulled the coupons and yes, some customers did get angry and stopped coming. But labor costs went down and most importantly, gross profitability went up. Over time, with some strategic promotion, we were able to rebuild the business with full price or *reasonably* discounted business. I know it's scary but I also know you didn't go into business to work for free.

In the case of the ink cartridge company, we didn't eliminate the delivery service, we just managed it better. The owners created a delivery schedule three mornings per week. They were able to schedule staff properly and make the deliveries in an orderly fashion. It was a reasonable alternative to the on-demand schedule.

For the Mother of the Bride store, we had to retrain the sales staff who operated in fear they would upset or turn off a customer. We simply set a time limit of one hour for visitors who came without an appointment. If, at the end of the hour, the sales associate sensed the guest was indecisive or just needed attention, they were trained to say, *"It seems you are going to need more time to make your decision. I'm going to suggest making an appointment at another time so I can give you my undivided attention. I am here on Tuesday and Thursday. Which is better for you?" Rather than leaving the customer feeling rejected, it enforced the credibility of the salesperson as an in-demand advisor who took their customer's satisfaction seriously.*

Remember, your job is to reward good customer behavior. Where are badly trained customers eating into your business? Don't be afraid to make a plan to retrain or replace them.

An alliance might consist of these strategies:

- Cross promoting on each other's websites and in social media
- Putting an offer on your receipts or including a flyer with each purchase
- Placing ads in each other's newsletters
- Offering a discount at your store when they make a purchase at the other
- Create joint emails, joint ads or even joint promotions

Reward your partners for sending new clients. The key to making this work is to have a tracking mechanism and to continually communicate with your partners. Send them monthly emails to let them know about new merchandise or sales. Visit them regularly so your store stays top of mind. An alliance needs to be nurtured so your partner is as vested in your success as you are in theirs.

I've had clients offer free services or benefits to managers and employees of neighboring stores. By familiarizing them with your great product or service, they are able to recommend you without hesitation because they've experienced it themselves.

Look right in your back yard. Your shopping center neighbors are great potential partners due to their close proximity or their natural correlation with your business.

I worked with a preschool that was having trouble getting enrollments. In visiting them, I realized they had a kid's hair salon, a pediatric dentist and a toy store all within their shopping center. These were the perfect alliance partners who all benefited from a formal program.

I've had beauty salons partner with plastic surgeons (a gift bag after every procedure with an offer for a makeover. What a great opportunity to bring someone in who is ripe for changing their look!) boutiques partner with dry cleaners who stapled their tags to every cleaning bag and restaurants that offered a free dessert for every customer of their partner's store.

In understanding the makeup of your best customers, think about potential partners and allies in your shopping center and neighborhood. Where can you best tap into a ready-made audience of prospects!

ACTION ITEM # 13
The People Factor
Answer these questions on the worksheet

I don't have a customer loyalty program but think it would help my business.

If you have a customer loyalty program, do you measure the residual results?

Is it producing the desired results?

Do you need to modify your existing program by:
      Additional/better marketing
      Additional/better benefits

Badly trained customers
This is an issue in my store that needs to be addressed.

Identify three potential strategic alliance partners for your business. What type of cross promotion can you organize with these partners that will benefit both businesses?

CHAPTER 19

Customer Service

Elevated service is one of the major reasons customers patronize independent retailers. Otherwise, they could easily go to a large store, find their own products, wait in line to pay and return items seemingly a decade after purchase. If you can't provide a better experience they have little reason to patronize you. Here's the bottom line: customers buy more when they're happy and feel valued. It's up to you and your staff to insure they're ecstatic!

Consider this. According to a Timetrade survey:
- When customers are assisted by a knowledgeable salesperson in a store, there's an 80 percent chance sales will increase by 25 percent to 50 percent.
- 80 percent of customers won't wait more than 5 minutes for service. They will leave if they can't find an item, if the line is too long or if they can't get an answer in that time.

Here's one more stat from a 2012 Accenture survey:

- 73 percent of customers believe they know more than retail employees.

Wow! These customer attitudes, along with the fact that consumer expectations of the in-store experience are elevating to new heights, make it easy to understand that excellence in customer service is a distinguishing factor in bricks and mortar success. It's what makes the cash register ring.

Training sales associates to offer a great big "Hello" when someone enters your store is hardly a customer service strategy. It's kind of the same thing as asking, "Are you looking for anything special?" (When I hear this I get really snarky and say, "No, I'm looking for something *un*special," I know, I should keep my mouth shut but it's truly the dumbest question ever!)

Here's another one I love:

"Can I help you find something?"

Yes, I'd like this in a size small.

Oh, everything we have is already out.

What! Why are you bothering me?

And finally, just today, I went into a big box office supply store which shall remain nameless. They had a greeter who actually asked me this question, *"What brings you to _____ today?"* I think the look on my face said it all and she actually backed away.

Your store greeting sets the tone. I once went into a clothing store where the associate said to me, *"Can I help you find something or are you just enjoying browsing?"* What a positive spin that allowed me the opportunity to say something positive back to her – "I'm enjoying browsing, thank you."

There are hundreds of books on customer service techniques. Take a look at your operation and see what might be lacking. Is checkout taking too long? Is merchandise not clearly priced? Are your sales people simply polite or do they have each and every customer's best interest at heart – even the difficult ones?

If you do nothing else, work on a proprietary greeting that differentiates your store. If I owned an art supply store, I'd have my associates say, *"What can we help you create today?"* For a cupcake or candy store, *"How can we make your life a little sweeter today?"* As corny as it may seem, these types of greetings disarm people, make them smile and deflect their defenses. They become more open to the possibility of purchasing from you.

Elevating the level of customer service in your store involves a number of things:

- Having enough associates to handle traffic and checkout
- Having well-trained associates (this goes back to making quality hires and training them properly)
- Knowing your customers and what they want. What's important to them? What type of shopping experience do they value? High level service? Speedy checkout? A deep selection? Convenience?
- A solid understanding of your brand and how that translates to the in-store experience

The top 9 customer service sins
1. Making a customer wait to pay
2. Associates chatting on cell phones, texting or talking about a customer
3. Not having the customer's best interest at heart
4. Not suggesting alternatives/upselling
5. Ignoring a customer
6. Not resolving complaints quickly and to the customer's satisfaction
7. Little or no product knowledge
8. Not validating the customer's purchase *("This is a great gift,"* or *"You're going to love using this.")*
9. Pre-judging the customer's desire or ability to buy

Overdoing it

There's a dark side to increased customer service and that's over-communicating and hovering. Here's an example I recently experienced with a doctor's office. I called and made an appointment two weeks out.

> I received an email confirmation that day. A text confirmation as well.
>
> I received a call from the office one week before the appointment and then two days before. I received a text the day before requiring I confirm my appointment and another one the day of the visit. Finally, 15 minutes before the appointment, while I was in the parking lot, I got a pre-recorded call that said if I wasn't there on time my appointment would be cancelled and I would be charged. Enough!

Here's the thing about customer service. You can read the books. You can bring in trainers. You can have a policy handbook three inches thick. But unless you hire people who actually love what they do, it will be all for naught. Hire people who like people. Hire people who want the best for the customer. Empower your employees to create customer satisfaction. If you do that, and you commit to creating an exceptional experience for everyone who walks in your door, you won't ever have to worry about it again. It's really that simple.

Secret Shoppers

Want an outside opinion on how your sales staff is performing? Try having them shopped. Although widely used in the retail world, most small operators don't usually access secret shopper services and they can be a real eye opener. For a relatively small fee – somewhere around $125-$200, you can have your associates shopped and evaluated. Do this quarterly and let your staff know it could happen at any time.

Last impressions

Much is made of first impressions but it's the experience a customer has in the last few minutes in your store that sticks with them. In addition to making people wait to pay, here are some things that happen that could have a customer leaving on a bad note:

- An employee who isn't able to work the POS properly
- Careless treatment of the purchased product
- Not saying goodbye and thank you

One of the best last impressions ever was delivered by a restaurant manager that came to the table and instead of asking the usual, "Was everything ok?" she said, "I hope you enjoyed yourself tonight. Was there anything we could have done better?"

I experienced another fantastic last impression at a nail salon. When the manicure was finished and I was sitting at the nail drying machine, the manicurist came over and rubbed my back and shoulders. Heaven!

You build trust with excellence. You build loyalty with excellence. Sure, everyone slips up now and again but if your overall service experience is positive, your customers will tend to be more forgiving of mistakes.

ACTION ITEM # 14

Customer Service

Evaluate your customer service on the worksheet.

My staff is knowledgeable and well-trained in:
       Customer engagement
       POS system operation/checkout
       Suggestive selling/upselling
       Product knowledge/benefits
       Store policies

I receive very few customer complaints of any kind.

CHAPTER 20

Two More Things To Think About

Vertical marketing

In taking a page from the business-to-business world, vertical marketing – targeting specific niche groups - is an incredible way to keep marketing costs low and impact high. The objective is to find a group of people who match your customer profile and infiltrate that community. This is an extremely targeted approach that allows you to get to know the influencers in that group and earn their trust.

I developed a marketing strategy for a chiropractor that focused on two vertical markets of people whose work kept them on their feet – retail workers and hair stylists. Due to the nature of their work, they experience a lot of back pain and stiffness. By making presentations in hair salons and at retail stores, offering free assessments and tips for keeping feet, legs, back and neck healthy, the doctor created buzz in those communities by offering solutions to their specific problems and earned their trust to build his business.

Think about a niche market for your business. Examples include: military veterans, moms, ethnic markets, the LBGT community, business women, brides and college students, to name a few. How can you market specifically to meet the needs of your chosen group and become their preferred provider or brand?

Product trials and sampling

From diapers to hamburgers to toothpaste, marketers know the power of free trials. Large companies spend millions to get their products into your hands in the hopes you will try them, like them and ultimately buy them. The same techniques hold true for your business. This is particularly true for eating establishments. I encourage my clients, whether they sell ice cream or fine foods, to post staff outside their doors daily with free samples of food for passersby, accompanied, of course, with bouncebacks as an incentive to purchase.

ACTION ITEM #15

Answer these questions on the worksheet.

Vertical marketing

Reaching out to the following niche markets would benefit my business:

1.

2.

3.

Are product trials and sampling applicable to your business?

If so, do you believe you could benefit from implementing a trial or sampling program?

So now what?

You've absorbed a lot of information in this MARKETING module and have evaluated the opportunities on your worksheet. While it can be overwhelming, the important thing to remember is to choose a few options and work them consistently. Marketing your establishment can be a fun and creative outlet. Don't be afraid to try new things. And don't be discouraged if they don't work. Just keep moving forward. Marketing is a daily part of your business success. Even the most well-known brands in the world need to reinforce their messages every single day. For the small retail or restaurant owner, it takes thought, creativity and a strong desire to bring – and keep - your business at the forefront.

MODULE #3
MEASURE

Chapter 21

Test. Measure. Tweak. Repeat.

Measurement is the linchpin of the entire growing small process. Here's where all your hard work comes together. So far, you've learned that you are in control of your business and its ultimate success. You've learned the best ways to manage and market your business. The next – and final- step is to measure the outcomes resulting from the money and effort you put into growing small. The information you need to transform and move forward exists and all you have to do is track it! And by measuring, I don't mean just top line sales growth. I mean every detail. This is the last piece of the puzzle and, unfortunately, the piece that's generally ignored.

When a client tells me about a program or campaign they've done in the past, the first thing I ask is, "What were the results?" I get this response way too often: *"We got a handful of sales out of it."* There's nothing more infuriating for me or more wasteful for the client.

Wouldn't you want to know exactly the return you got for your hard work?

Remember the breakfast restaurant I talked about earlier? We started a kid's program that offered a free breakfast special for children with the purchase of an adult meal. At the end of the first month, I asked the client for the results. I got the "handful" response so I asked them to pull the sales by category for the month. Turns out, they experienced a 10 percent increase in the special which means the flyer they were using was working. Numbers are powerful tools!

When you've finished this book and executed your plan, it is my goal that you will know EXACTLY what is working for you and, just as importantly, what isn't.

The ability to measure will give you the confidence to try new things. In the book, *Fail Fast. Fail Often: How Losing Can Help You Win*, the author says, "Successful people understand that the best way to learn about something and get good at it is to fail at it is as fast as they can." The book also talks about how Silicon Valley entrepreneurs call the effort "falling forward." In the tech world, they just keep plugging along through each failure until they get it right. Similarly, in sales, we work on the "no" system. When you know your closing ratio, say, 1 in 10, you know you need 9 no's to get to a yes. So every "no" actually becomes a celebration because it's getting you one step closer to that yes. Failure is simply a stepping stone to success.

There are two important lessons here:
1. By understanding that failure is part of the process you become fearless. You are free to experiment and, in general,

be more innovative knowing that if it doesn't work, no harm, no foul. Don't let missteps trip you up. Learn and move on.

2. Nobody knows everything. We all have to learn and that's okay. We will learn from every initiative we implement and build upon the results of each.

Tips for measuring

Anything you do can and should be measured. You probably understand how to measure your email open rate and the redemption percentages of your coupons but we're going to take it far beyond that. And if you can't measure it, you might not want to do it.

Attach a goal to every initiative. If it's a first time program, guestimate a reasonable goal. If you've done it before, increase the goal and determine what tweaks you'll need to make to improve performance and results. NOTE: Don't change too many variables in a program at a time, just one or two so you can accurately determine what's actually working -or not.

Chapter 22

The What, When and How of Measuring

Where to start
We already discussed monitoring KPI's regularly in the MANAGE
Module. The information you gather will give you the baseline or
jumping off point for your marketing decisions.

Measuring sales
Measure and track sales weekly and compare to year-over-year
results. Next drill down deeper and compare sales by category. Look
for patterns that indicate changes in the product mix you're selling.
A restaurant, for example, would track sales by lunch and dinner and
then by category of items sold during the two parts of the day. They
would also measure catering and delivery if applicable.

Is there a category that's weakening? Or one that represents a growth
opportunity? Is there a consistently underperforming product or

category that you can eliminate that might free up cash flow and allow you to purchase or expand a more lucrative piece of your business?

The makeup store I mentioned earlier had a very deep inventory of products and was spending quite a bit monthly on bringing in new products and restocking to keep inventory fresh. In examining their sales by category, we determined the majority of their sales were coming from just twenty or so items. By knowing that, they were able to reduce inventory spending by 14 percent and still maintain sales levels.

By understanding sales by category you are also able to create a growth strategy by specific category rather than an overall monthly number. A restaurant might choose to focus on dinner appetizers or catering; a dry cleaner on large household items like quilts and drapes. It's easier to target and grow a specific niche then create a blanket overall revenue growth strategy.

You'll also measure sales by employee and track performance based on any incentive-based program you decide to implement. If you decide not to create an incentive program but do implement a training program – which I hope you will – track sales by employee for individual improvement.

I conducted a fun experiment with a Japanese restaurant recently. The staff was mediocre at best. It wasn't their fault. They had never had any training. I wanted to teach them how to upsell and how that could affect their tips. So I gave them a simple line to use at every table. "I'll give you some time to look at the menu. In the meantime, can I bring an order of edamame for the table?" I chose the edamame because it's universally popular and at this restaurant, was just $5 per order. At the end of the first *month, edamame sales doubled! In calculating the numbers, I was able to show the servers, based on a 20 percent tip, they had each earned an extra $40 that month. By translating that revenue increase into tips they could potentially be earning by upselling drinks and higher priced items, I got their attention.*

Long term tracking
We need to get away from the transactional mentality and begin measuring sales from new customers that come from a specific source over a period of time.

Let's use an in-store promotion or a daily deal special as an example (if you do a daily deal please be sure to collect an email address for everyone who redeems a coupon!). Code new customers from these promotions by lead source in your database. Now, analyze them as a separate group the same way you would existing customers – by average sale, products purchased, zip code, gender, etc. Then compare that to your existing client database to see if a particular campaign or promotion brought in customers that exhibited different buying patterns.

Now, let's say that promotion cost $2500 in hard costs and the resulting "day-of" sales were only $1000. Not a great ROI. Don't despair. In addition to strategizing what you might do to get a better outcome from future promotions, continue to track this database segment for the next 12 months and see what the value of the group is over the course of a year. If you continue your email marketing campaign to this customer group, you may see that you realized $5,000 in sales from that segment which will have been an excellent return on your investment. The value of marketing doesn't have to be immediate to be impactful.

Sales per square foot

Track sales per square foot (PSF) and benchmark them against sales for stores in your category. You can research these statistics on the Internet or through trade associations. In addition, track sales PSF for display areas to see if you're effectively featuring the correct merchandise and deals within your store.

Measure the square footage of your displays and each time you create a new one, track the sales of the items on that display against the square footage of the display. So if your display takes up 10 square feet and you sell $1000 worth of items featured on that display, your sales PSF for the display would be $100. This number should be higher than the sales PSF for the overall store. Your goal should be to continually increase the sales PSF in your display areas.

If you create a new window display, track sales of the items in the window and also compare traffic with each new window. Is the new window generating more interest – and traffic – to your store?

As you start making changes to your store experience, from signage to music, do them one at a time and track sales. It would be interesting to confirm whether or not a change in lighting or music or scent led to increased sales or, at minimum, positive customer reaction. Or if a new selection of items at your cash wrap are responsible for a bump in your average sale. Always try something new, no matter how small, and track it. These little experiments prove how small changes can make a big difference and will motivate you to continue tweaking.

AB Testing for media, direct mail, email and coupons
AB testing is simply a matter of testing two offers or variables against each other – version A and version B – at the same time. It's an amazing and no-cost way to see what messages, subject lines and offers resonate best with your audience.

Next time you send out an email, test a single variable – let's say, the subject line. Don't send it out to your entire database, just a representative sample. See which version gets a better open rate, then you can send out the more successful email to the balance of your database. Utilize AB testing in all your advertising and couponing on an ongoing basis. If you find a message or offer that works better, test it against another message. There are always ways to improve performance and response, thereby getting better value for your marketing efforts.

Online analytics
Most online platforms offer free analytics to help you track performance. This incredibly useful information will provide you with solid data from which to make future plans. For our purposes, I am going to review the analytics available primarily through free programs, however, should you wish to go deeper into tracking and measuring, there are paid programs available, including platforms that will provide metrics for all your social media in one place.

Google analytics for your website
Virtually one hundred percent of the clients I've worked with never took the time to learn who, if anyone, was visiting their website. That's unfortunate since Google analytics is a free tool to help you learn more about your website and how to improve it.

Go to google.com/analytics to set up your account. The process is easy but you may have to call in a pro to insert the code onto your pages that allows for tracking. Be sure to have them code every page. Once set up, it may take about 24 hours for the program to start providing information.

Your Google analytics dashboard gives you:

Visits – number of people who visited the site

Page views - how many times the pages on your website have been viewed

Pages/visit – the average number of pages someone visits while on your site

Bounce rate – the percentage of users who left your site after visiting only one page

Average time on site – how long people are staying

New visits – the number of people who have never visited your site before

Map overlay – shows the geographic location of your visitors. You can drill down by country, state and even city.

Traffic source – How are visitors getting to your site? From a search engine, by putting your URL in their browser, from a referral link?

Content overview – the most viewed pages

Day and time stats –track when visitors are coming to your site

Search terms – the keywords people are using to find your site

By analyzing your website usage, you are able to learn more about viewing habits, track the performance of new content, see which pages are getting the most traction, review your geographic reach and better optimize your site with the most popular keywords.

Social Media

Most social media platforms provide these basic metrics:

Reach -the number of unique people or visitors to see your post or ad.

Impressions -the actual number of times your post or ad is viewed. Impressions may be higher than reach due to multiple views by the same person.

Engagement -the number and percentage of people who commented on or like your posts.

Using these simple metrics, you can analyze any specific post to see the number of impressions and then calculate the percentage of people who engaged by commenting or liking. Look for patterns in the type of posts that are getting a higher engagement. What is it about them that's resonating with your followers? These analytics are always available online but most platforms also allow you to export all the information to an Excel spreadsheet for ongoing tracking and comparisons.

Facebook

Facebook offers a suite of analytics accessible right from your home page. At the top left, click on Insights. Here is all the reporting you'll need to analyze the performance of your posts and the makeup of your audience available by the week or any other specified date range you choose.

Not only will you find total engagement and reach, you can track likes, shares and clicks by each specific post. You'll be able to analyze the performance of difference types of posts (those with photos, videos and links). Facebook Insights also provides information on followers by gender, age and location and time of visit as well. You can also track the origin of your visits; whether or not they come from a Google search, your website, an email or other source.

Facebook also gives you suggested pages to follow and if you choose to do so, will provide information on the posts from those pages as well. Everything Facebook tracks is segmented by organic vs. paid to show you how your paid promotion is performing.

Twitter

Twitter's free analytics are a bit more difficult to find. You'll have to go to www.analytics.twitter.com and sign up for Twitter ads. This involves giving them a credit card, however you don't have to purchase any ads. Just by doing this you'll have access to analytics that provide impressions, engagements, Tweet replies, link clicks and your averages for these metrics, both paid and organic, over a 30 day period or selected date range.

You Tube

You Tube also provides its own free analytics information that tracks the number of views, estimated minutes watched, subscribers, likes, dislikes, comments shared, geographic and gender information and top traffic sources. Click on My Channel in the upper left side of your page to access.

Instagram

Instagram recently announced the availability of analytics for advertisers, but doesn't currently offer tools for general users. There are, however, several resources for free analytics including Iconosquare (www.iconosquare.com) and Simply Measured (www. simplymeasured.com).

Pinterest

Pinterest's analytics require providing a website domain on your profile which needs to be verified. Once that's done, you'll be able to access your analytics from the top right hand corner. The tool provides impressions, volume (activity/people), recent pins, most-repinned images and which pins drive the most visits to your website.

Email

Your email provider (i.e. Constant Contact) provides complete analytics for your email campaigns. The analytics will help you understand:

- Who is opening your email
- Who is clicking on the links inside your email
- Who is forwarding your email

Email analytics include:

Bounce rate – number of emails not delivered usually because the email address was incorrect. If your email database is out of date, you'll probably have a high bounce rate. Your email provider will give you a report of which emails bounced and if it doesn't automatically do it for you, you'll need to delete these emails so you have a good, clean database.

Delivery rate -the number of emails that actually landed in the recipients mail box (total number of emails sent less the number that bounced).

Unique open rate – the number of people who viewed your email one time.

Open rate- the total number of times your email was viewed.

Unsubscribe – the number of recipients who opted out.

Click through rate – the number of people who took action by clicking on a link in the email. This could include forwards, website links, social media links or links to articles and blogs.

Track the performance of each email you send. Consider the AB testing option mentioned earlier so you can consistently improve your email metrics. If you are providing an offer in an email, track response to the offer and against the open rate of the email itself to see what percentage of people reading the email are actually taking advantage of the offer. This type of tracking takes just a few minutes and will help you maximize the impact of your email marketing program.

Media/Branding campaigns/PR

These types of campaigns cannot be directly tracked to sales but you can track phone calls, store traffic and website visits over the course of the campaign. Of course, you can also look at your overall sales during the campaign to see if there's a bump. Owners generally don't track the number of phone calls received during the day but it's a great idea to get a benchmark average and then track that against calls received when running a branding campaign.

Bouncebacks/Referral cards/Coupons

Two common mistakes I see with these tools is failure to measure sales relative to the offer as well as the redemption percentage based on the number distributed.

The first thing you need to do is code each bounceback or card to the source. So, if you're doing sampling outside your store on Friday, May 13th, you need to code that bounceback to the date. If you are giving referral cards to staff members to distribute, you need to code them back to that staff member.

Next, keep track of the number of cards you hand out in a particular timeframe, for example, during your May 13th sampling, you distributed 56 bouncebacks.

Finally, track the redemption. If the May 13th sampling produced 10 redemptions, you'll know you earned a nearly 18 percent redemption rate on your effort. You'll also want to track the value of the redeemed bouncebacks. If those 10 cards redeemed produced $90 worth of sales, (you can staple a copy of the receipt to each card) you now have a benchmark and can work to create programs with higher redemption rates as well as sales volumes.

If you're using staff-distributed referral cards as a marketing tool, keeping track of them as described above is an excellent means of determining whether or not a particular staff member is fully participating in the program.

Bouncebacks and referral cards are also an excellent opportunity to try AB testing to see which offers are producing more results.

Loyalty programs

Your loyalty program should be monitored and measured for effectiveness. The goal is not just to get members but to produce sales and engagement.

Here, you'll want to measure not just the signups but the actual usage of the program benefits. Track:

- Number of new members joining monthly
- Percentage of members purchasing monthly
- Percentage of members actually redeeming the offers

Again, testing new and different offers to see if they improve signups and/or redemption rates is the key.

Alliances and partnerships

Each time you create a partnership with an organization or business, you'll want to track the productivity of that partnership on both sides - what that partnership is bringing to your store and what your store is delivering. Remember, these partnerships only work if both parties benefit.

If your partner is handing out referral cards, be sure those cards are coded so you can track them back. The same goes for any you hand out on their behalf. Whatever your partnership entails, whether it's placing ads in your newsletters or distributing flyers, all partners should actively track results in order to keep the motivation to actively participate high.

As you create your plan you'll be including a measurement goal and device with each element. I can't say it enough times: the more you know about the success or failure of your efforts, the more effective and valuable your marketing efforts can be. As CEO of your company, you should expect and demand performance in all areas of your business.

CHAPTER 23

Creating The Plan

It's time to put the pot on boil and create your own 90-day plan for growing small! If you've followed along with the worksheet while reading, you're almost there! If you haven't, take some time to go back and put some thought into the Building Blocks and Action Items exercises. When finished, you should have a clear idea of your priorities.

A few things to remember as you move forward:
1. The key to creating a viable plan is to keep it focused and simple.
2. Start by addressing any critical infrastructural issues identified in the Building Block exercises.
3. Your plan should contain no more than 5-10 items depending on the complexity and amount of work necessary to complete each. Regardless of how many things you'd like to tackle, start with the priorities. You'll get the best results when you

concentrate on excellent execution of a few elements. Be realistic about the time commitment you'll be able to devote so as not to end up frustrated.

4. Once you've completed the first 90-day plan, evaluate your success then create a second plan that includes tweaks to round one and add new elements that will help you get closer to your ultimate goals.

Note: Use the downloaded plan template as a guide. It contains all the options reviewed in the book but you'll only select those areas that pertain to you.

Must do's

Regardless of which priorities you choose for your plan, it must contain the following:

Tracking Key Performance Indicators – All the KPI's pertinent to your business need to be tracked and monitored weekly.

Managing yourself – include at least one personal growth item as part of the plan.

Social media – choose at least one platform to incorporate into your marketing strategy.

Email marketing – even if you already have a program in place, create techniques to improve the performance and effectiveness of your email marketing.

Monitoring/managing your online reviews – this is
a critical part of today's marketing and needs to be
consistently addressed.

Step one

Complete Building Blocks 1-5 and insert answers on the worksheet.

The building blocks deal with the infrastructure of your business. As
we discussed, you need to build a strong foundation from which to
grow small. It's important to finish these items first. If you decide, for
example, to change your concept, then your first 90-day plan would
center around implementing those conceptual changes.

Building Block # 1

This is an assessment of your business and management skills. Note
all the items you've checked as "True." These are potential red flags
to be considered. Prioritize and list them on the plan template along
with your top 3 business issues.

Review your answers under the "What do you want to achieve
section?"

List these answers as long term goals. Write in your long term
personal and business financial goals as well. This is what you'll
ultimately be working towards and it's a good idea to always have
them handy as you create your plan.

Building Block # 2
Your concept

Have you clearly defined your concept? Do you plan on tweaking or changing it? If you are going to make modifications, now is the time to do it and create your plan around the framework of the new idea. If your store concept needs improvement/change or modification or the physical representation of the concept needs improvement, this should be a priority in round one.

Building Block # 3
Brand evaluation

Your brand message is the foundation of your marketing and may need to be created or modified before you can continue. If anything in your physical store or marketing message is detracting from your brand, these items should also be addressed in the initial plan.

Building Block #4
The Point of Sale (POS) system

Since so much of managing your business is dependent on the POS you will either need to:

1. Do your research on the purchase of a POS system for your business and buy one OR create a system for manually tracking key information.
2. Arrange to begin inputting the proper information that will make your POS a functioning tool
3. Get training on how to access reports from your existing POS system.
4. If you have a POS, input the proper information and know how to pull reports, decide which Key Performance indicators

will be most beneficial to your business and beginning pulling and analyzing those reports for benchmark comparisons.

Whichever step applies to you, write that into the template.

Building Block # 5
Creating the customer profile

This is the final building block. Without a clear idea of your target customer, the development of your marketing strategy will be random and likely less effective.

Step two

If you have not already done so, complete the Action Item exercises on the worksheet. Here's a quick review.

MANAGE MODULE

Action item #1

A personal assessment of the aspects of business ownership you like and dislike as well as a rating of your skill level in key management areas. List the areas you dislike and/or need to either improve or outsource on the template. Focus on those marked as urgent in the plan. You can either choose to work on areas that need improvement or outsource them. Be strategic in these decisions. For example, if you are not good at hiring, you will probably have to get some training in this area and continue to do it yourself. If there's a deficiency in social media on the other hand, it might be worth your while to hire someone to take care of it.

Regardless of how many areas may need to be addressed, prioritize and choose the top one or two for your first 90-day plan.

Action item #2

This exercise is simply to help you identity brand attributes that might be applicable to your store/brand and assist you in creating a stronger, more resonant message.

Action item #3

Do you have any employee issues that need to be dealt with immediately? Would employee training and or an incentive program better help you reach your sales goals?

Action item #4

You must commit to at least one personal growth item as part of your plan.

MARKETING MODULE

If you don't have a professionally created logo that works well on all platforms, logo creation should be a part of your initial plan.

Action item #5

Is the competition affecting your business? If so, create a system for gathering and/or better organizing of competitive intelligence.

Action item #6

What needs immediate attention in your store? Cleanliness? Lighting? Merchandising? Window displays? Phone protocols? Do you need to modify or change your store appearance to work better with your brand or concept? Put any items that need immediate attention on the first 90-day plan.

Action item #7

List the areas of your website that need improvement. Are you able to make those changes yourself or do you need to hire someone? Is there a budget? If you can make the improvements yourself or if you have a budget, is the upgrading/improving of your website something that should be addressed immediately or down the road?

Action item #8

After reading this chapter on social media and reviewing the various platforms, choose the top one or two platforms you would like to create a strategy around. This is a must.

Action item #9

Decide whether or not Pay Per Click (PPC) advertising or online sales make sense for your particular business at this time.

Monitoring and managing your online reviews must be on your plan either as a startup activity or for regular monitoring.

Action item #10

Evaluate advertising channels as well as your budget, if any. Determine whether or not you should enter into this arena now, or in the future. If you currently utilize traditional advertising, evaluate its effectiveness and create a strategy to improve it, if necessary.

An email marketing campaign must be on your plan.

Action item #11

What kind of promotions are you currently doing? Are you measuring their effectiveness? Should you add additional promotions to your marketing strategy? At minimum, you should create an annual promotional calendar to include participation in Small Business Saturday and Independent Business month.

Action item # 12

Would you benefit from hiring a public relations firm or trying to tackle some local PR pitches? Perhaps it's time to research local bloggers that might help publicize your business.

Action item #13

Do you have a customer loyalty program? If so, do you measure the results? Is it time to modify or improve the program?

Are badly trained customers an issue for your store?

Who are potential strategic partners that can help grow your business? What type of cross promotion plan can you develop that will be of benefit to you and your partners?

Action item # 14

Evaluate your store's customer service and determine, what, if anything, needs improvement.

Action item #15

Consider any vertical or niche markets that might give you a marketing edge. Would trials or sampling be an effective way to introduce your product to consumers?

Step three
Create the goals

What do you want to accomplish in the next three months? Write
down those goals on the worksheet. There should be no more than
3- 5 goals on your initial plan and they should be very specific and
measurable. For example, if increasing revenue by 10 percent is a goal,
you should be specific as to how you intend to achieve the increase.
Here are a few examples:

> Increase restaurant sales by 10 percent through an
> increase in dinner business or catering.

> Increase store sales by 10 percent by increasing sales
> per employee.

> Increase average sale by ___% which would result in
> an overall increase of revenue of 10 percent.

> Increase sales conversion rate by _____ which will
> results in a revenue increase of 10 percent.

Not all goals will - or should - be revenue based. They must be,
nonetheless, measurable. For example, you might decide on goals
like:

> Increase email database by_____and
> implement a twice monthly email campaign achieving
> a 20 percent open rate.

Increase Facebook "likes" by 200 and post engagement rate by 20 percent.

Step four

Now write the 5-10 items you want to include in your first 90-day plan. For each goal, select the items on the plan that will help you achieve that goal. For example, if you want to increase sales by creating and implementing a staff incentive program, that would go in the staff strategy section. Next, outline the specific implementation steps or tactics. Write down the person responsible for each step, a deadline date for each and budget, if applicable. Steps might include:

1. Create the incentive plan framework
2. Introduce program to staff
3. Meet individually with each staff member to discuss goals
4. Weekly training of staff (include training dates and agenda)
5. Review of sales vs. goal with each staff member (twice monthly)

Here's another example of steps for an email marketing program:

1. Determine topics, tone for the emails
2. Create email template
3. Decide who will write and produce the content
4. Schedule email dates
5. Will you perform A/B testing?

Step five

In the last column of the plan, insert your measurement metric. In the first example above, the measurement might be an overall increase of 8 percent in sales by employees. For the email program, it could be achieving a 20 percent open rate and a 15 percent redemption rate on special offers included in the email (if any).

In another instance where you might be distributing bouncebacks as part of your strategy, your goal might be a 30 percent redemption rate. Now many of these ideas you are trying may be new to your business and you don't have a basis for comparison. Just make an educated guess and try to meet that goal. In the case of bouncebacks, for example, think about the part of this program you can control, the actual distribution. So decide that you want to distribute a minimum of 200 bouncebacks. As you monitor distribution, count the number of bouncebacks you are distributing daily and stay on track. If you're falling behind, come up with a contingency plan for distribution. This is the benefit of consistent monitoring of your implementation in order to guarantee hitting key milestones.

Step five

Now it's time to do the work and monitor the progress. Decide how you will manage the plan. Will you review the list for a few minutes at the beginning of each day to insure you stay on track? Or have a weekly staff meeting to monitor progress? Whatever works best for you, be sure to schedule that time as a non-negotiable appointment with yourself!

Remember the creation and implementation of a plan for success doesn't have to be complicated. It does have to be well-thought out and organized. The more detailed the plan, the easier it will be to implement. The tracking devices not only keep you on target, they keep you motivated to continue. You are now on your way to creating transformative change one step at a time!

CHAPTER 24

Before You Sign That Lease!

If you haven't started your business yet, this is a great time to NOT make some common mistakes and position yourself for a truly successful start. Here are a few tips and words of wisdom for launching your new retail store or restaurant.

Choosing a location
Finding your store or restaurant location is an exciting task and perhaps the most important first step. Choosing the right storefront can make a huge difference in your future business and should be considered thoughtfully.

Your Space
Don't take more space than you need. Don't be seduced by a cheaper rent and the ability to take a larger space figuring you'll "grow" into it. Better to spend the money on a right size space in a better location.

Plus, it costs more money to effectively merchandise and stock a larger store.

Frontage

How much street or parking lot visibility does the location provide? The more, the better.

Room for the essentials

In addition to your displays and checkout, do you have enough room to build out an accessible and sufficient storage area? A small seating area? An employee break room? An office if you think you'll need one?

Parking

Is there sufficient parking in the center? Be sure to visit at various times of day to observe different parking patterns. If the location you're considering is near a movie theater or popular restaurant, for example, the parking lot may be full in the evenings and on weekends making it difficult for your customers to park.

Do the empanada math

I coined this after working with an empanada restaurant that opened in a 3000+ square foot space in the elbow of a shopping center in a suburban strip mall. At $4 an empanada, they needed to sell an awful lot to pay the $6000 monthly rent and that particular location fell short on the traffic necessary to do so. It was a problem that could have been avoided if they had just done the empanada math which simply means hanging out at the prospective location for a day or two and watch the traffic patterns. Is there enough volume of traffic to support your business? This simple test can prevent you from making a huge mistake!

Complimentary neighbors

Finding a location near stores that draw the same target as yours is a great bonus. If you are opening a women's shoe store, you'd want to find a center with women's boutiques and salons. For a children's store, look for businesses that draw moms, like a pediatric or OB/GYN practice, a children's gym or a preschool.

Competition

Is there competition in the center? That's not necessarily a bad thing if your concept is well defined and mixes well with the existing tenants. Will you be at the highest end or the lowest? One thing you don't want to do is locate somewhere where you'll just be fighting for the same dollar as your competitors. For example, if you want to open an ice cream store in a center where there is already a bakery, a cupcake store and a frozen yogurt store, there are just too many players vying for the dessert dollar.

Do the center demographics sync with your concept?

Does the location fit nicely with the concept you're considering? You don't want to put your high end restaurant in a lower end neighborhood.

Your Lease

The lease application

Fill out the leasing package your landlord requires thoughtfully, completely and accurately. This is the first real insight the landlord has about your business as they're considering you as a tenant and the more professional your lease application, especially if you're a first time operator, the better.

Buildouts

What, if any, concessions will the landlord give you in Tenant Improvement (TI) dollars. Is it sufficient to make the improvements necessary or will you have to add money to supplement?

Signage

One of the most common complaints I get across the board from tenants is they bemoan the fact the landlord won't give them signage on the shopping center pylon. Please note this is something that needs to be negotiated in your lease, not after the fact. But also note these signs are generally reserved only for larger tenants.

Be sure to understand your lease requirements for signage. Are you responsible for paying for overhead or other signage? Will you be included on directional signage, if any? What other signage is allowed?

Your lease will also identify other center restrictions like prohibiting sandwich boards, hours of operation requirements and parking restrictions. Be sure you are familiar with all your responsibilities, liabilities and restrictions so nothing comes as a surprise later on.

Hire a lawyer

Perhaps the biggest mistake new retailers make is neglecting to get a lawyer's advice on their lease. Remember, these are written to the advantage of the landlord and you should plan on investing in legal counsel to be sure you are protected and you know your rights and restrictions. A lawyer can also help you to fully understand the Common Area Maintenance (CAM) charges you'll pay each month, as well as when and how they might increase. When might you be in default? Are you responsible for sales tax, garbage or other fees that might increase your monthly budget? A lawyer experienced in lease review is worth every penny you will pay.

Business plan

Unless you are writing a business plan for the purpose of getting a loan or financing, you can do a simpler version for use as a roadmap to guide you through the start up and launch process. Use the business plan creation as an opportunity to fully think through every nuance of your business down to the last detail; from the kind of forms you'll need to the licenses required to the actual channels you'll use for marketing. Leave nothing to chance.

Aim to get as accurate a sense of expenses possible. Research typical start up and monthly costs for your type of business: labor, cost of goods sold, rent, marketing, gross margins, etc. You can find this information in abundance on the Internet or through your local small business development and SCORE center. Remember, these are just averages but it's a good place to start. Don't skimp on expenses. You *will* need marketing dollars. You *will* need a website. You *will* need a POS system. Don't count on paying for these things later, out of cash flow. You need to purchase the tools that will make your business successful in advance, not the other way around.

Will you need money to hire an architect? Lighting planner? How much will you allocate for displays and furniture?

Are you taking out a loan or borrowing from your 401k? If you are going to incur debt to start your business, be sure to figure that into your expenses and understand that the payback of a loan will delay profitability.

Be realistic about your revenue goals. The revenue projection in your plan is simply an educated guestimate. Don't just make up a number so that it covers expenses. Count on losing money for a while. Even if you have a fantastic first year, there's a very good chance you'll experience sophomore slump in year two. That doesn't mean you're a failure. It just means you're not the new kid on the block anymore.

Try to get a sense of what similar businesses in your area are doing in terms of annual revenue and/or the revenue trajectory of the stores in the center in which you're thinking of leasing. The landlord probably won't give you this information but talking to existing tenants might give you some insight.

When creating your business plan, it's a good time to take off your rose colored glasses and put on your devil's advocate cap. If you were to do 50 percent of what you projected in year one, would you make it?

Talk to other tenants in the center
Beware, talking to neighboring tenants might open a can of worms. Every center has disgruntled tenants who will tell you everything is wrong and may be playing the blame game with the landlord or the center. Talk to those who are doing well and those who aren't. Make your own judgments. Are the stores that claim they aren't doing well good concepts? What does your gut tell you?

Permitting

Often times, the landlord will give you free rent for several months to allow you time to build out your store. Time and time again, owners underestimate the amount of time it will take for construction and permitting and end up paying rent long before their store is open.

Starting your business is the most exciting time, full of hope and anticipation. Take the time to organize and contemplate everything that can get in the way of a stellar launch. Keep your CEO hat on at all times and, unless there's a great reason to do so, try not to be swayed from your original concept and vision.

Don't expect too much too soon. You'll find yourself being disappointed instead of motivated and you may put yourself in an unnecessary financial crunch.

You're about to enter into a great new adventure! Create your business on the most solid foundation possible and enjoy every minute of it!

CHAPTER 25

Final Thoughts on Growing Small

Congratulations on taking your future success in hand and your willingness to do the work necessary to achieve your goals. Not every owner is willing to do this so the fact that you're here means you're already well ahead of the pack.

There is no doubt there will be frustrations as you move forward. But there will also be moments of joy and accomplishment. Embrace those moments. Celebrate them.

Growing small is not a linear process. If you try something and it doesn't work, examine the execution. Was it a good idea that suffered from bad implementation? Is there a way to do it better? Always analyze and debrief on every project. Even if it doesn't work, you'll want to know why.

Keep one important thing in mind, though. In retail, the market determines your success. The market tells you what it wants and what it's willing to pay for it. It's that simple. So as you create and execute your plan, keep your eyes and ears on the people. Don't just listen to the people who love you. Listen to the people who don't like your idea. Most importantly, listen to the silence. If your store is empty – even after a good solid marketing push – listen. And rather than getting discouraged, make the changes necessary to give the market what it needs.

Don't be afraid to innovate. Today's retail is a sea of sameness. There's never been a better time, in my opinion, for someone large or small to transform the landscape. It can be you!

My final thought for you is a question. Do you believe? Do you believe in your concept? Yourself? The future of your business? You have to believe you can do this in order for it to work. So as you move forward, remember these words from Thomas Edison, "When you have exhausted all possibilities, remember this: you haven't."

Wishing you the best of luck.

Send us your success stories.
We'd love to hear how you used the Growing Small process to improve your business. Send your stories to success@growingsmall.co

About the Author

Angel has small business in her DNA! Based on her thirty-plus years of experience as a business owner and corporate executive in sales and marketing, she created a unique new platform to assist small retailers create thriving businesses.

Angel is the recipient of local, regional, and national awards for creative excellence and business ownership and a sought-after speaker and seminar leader.

The Growing Small Manifesto
Small business is the foundation of our economic machine. Let's focus on creating the best small business possible—not bigger, just better!

Printed in the United States
By Bookmasters